The
Hollywood
Storyteller

The
Hollywood
Storyteller

Mark Drop

Friedman Group

A FRIEDMAN GROUP BOOK

Copyright © 1992 by Michael Friedman Publishing Group, Inc.

ISBN 0-7924-5540-1

THE HOLLYWOOD STORYTELLER
was prepared and produced by
Michael Friedman Publishing Group, Inc.
15 West 26th Street
New York, New York 10010

Editor: Elizabeth Viscott Sullivan
Art Director: Jeff Batzli
Designer: Susan Livingston
Photography Editor: Grace How

Color separations by United South Sea Graphic Art Co.
Printed and bound in Hong Kong by Leefung-Asco Printers Ltd.

For Mimi.

I can never thank you enough for asking,

"What is it you want to do with your life?"

ACKNOWLEDGMENTS

Special thanks to Elizabeth Sullivan, my editor, for her well-placed blue pencil and stick-em notes, and to the Academy of Motion Picture Arts and Sciences Margaret Herrick Library in Beverly Hills, for its beautiful reading room and orderly shelves stocked with everything I needed to complete this book.

Contents

part one

The Cast

CHAPTER ONE

Welcome to Tinseltown

All great stories need a setting, a backdrop against which they can be played out. The stories included here happen to have one of the most exciting, colorful backdrops there is: Hollywood, U.S.A.

The history of Hollywood, and of the industry that grew up there, is the familiar story of a boomtown, repeated in many small towns throughout the West. The big difference between Hollywood and other western boomtowns is that Hollywood has endured while most of the others have withered into ghost towns.

Hollywood began as a quiet subdivision of Los Angeles, California, in 1887, when conservative Kansas prohibitionist Harvey Wilcox registered a map of his 120-acre (49-ha) citrus ranch with the Los Angeles County Recorder's Office and offered up plots for sale. He named the subdivision Hollywood after the country home of a woman his wife met on a train. Wilcox tried several times to grow holly on the property, but it always died.

Slowly the area grew, becoming sparsely populated by like-minded conservative midwesterners who came for the quiet and the climate.

While the mansions and lemon trees sprouted in Hollywood, a feverish quest continued back on the East Coast and in Europe to give detailed photographic images motion—as Thomas A. Edison said "to do for the eye what the phonograph has done for the ear."

Edison's mission to create moving pictures was successful, and by 1896 he held his first public screening—shots of everyday events and

Opposite: Cecil B. De Mille, sporting jodhpurs and riding boots, is the director's director as he lords over production of The Greatest Show on Earth. *Right: The moguls who gambled on sound and won: (left to right) William Konig, Darryl F. Zanuck, Jack Warner, Al Jolson, and Albert Warner.*

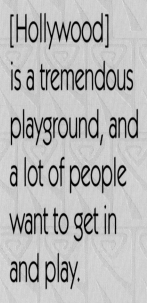

[Hollywood] is a tremendous playground, and a lot of people want to get in and play.

— Brian De Palma, director

crashing waves, which frightened nervous spectators. By the early 1900s, the novelty had caught on and crowds of urban immigrants in the East flocked to nickelodeons to see the "flickers." Back then, Chicago, Philadelphia, and New York were the centers of film production, distribution, and exhibition. But not for long.

Edison and the few companies producing movies at the time wanted desperately to hang on to the right to do so—and to the tremendous profits that came with it. They joined together to create the Patents Company, basically a monopoly to prevent competition among each other. Those outside the Patents Company not so lovingly called it the "Trust."

The Trust is often credited with driving filmmakers out West, beyond the reach of its lawyers and thugs. This is only partly true. In fact, several Trust members were among the first to take advantage of the area's perfect climate, cheap labor, and wide variety of shooting locations—beaches, mountains, thriving metropolises, and tiny villages. These first pioneers were foreign immigrants—men like Louis B. Mayer, Carl Laemmle, and Samuel Goldwyn—and out West, free to experiment and develop, they turned what had been a cottage industry into a massive production line.

But life was no bowl of oranges in Hollywood. The town had become a bastion of ultramoralists who held two activities to be truly corrupt: drinking and exhibiting moving pictures. Both doings were banned in Hollywood, which was still just a group of widely spaced farms. The streets were dirt trails, and even after 1910 the most efficient mode of transportation was horseback. Actors, too, were unwelcome and often barred from taking up residence. Consequently, the first of the larger studios sprang up around the outside of the township in Santa Monica, or over the hills in Universal City.

Even the great Cecil B. De Mille had troubles shooting the first picture to come out of Hollywood proper. Sent west in 1913 by Sam Goldwyn to shoot a western called The *Squaw Man*, De Mille was bound for Arizona but instead pushed on ahead to Hollywood. He probably wished he hadn't. During production he was shot at twice by angry residents. The first negative of his print was sabotaged, so he took to sleeping in the film lab to protect the duplicate. The town's attempts at stopping him notwithstanding, De Mille made it back to New York with the print that became a smash hit. *The Squaw Man*'s success ensured that Hollywood would ever after be synonymous with movies.

Above: Cinematic master D.W. Griffith genuflects before his biggest star, Mary Pickford, on the earliest type of sound-stage—the great outdoors.

The silent movies were vastly popular and spawned the first movie stars, Mary Pickford, Charlie Chaplin, Lillian Gish, and Theda Bara among them. The art of cinema continued to improve, most notably in director D. W. Griffith's epic films, *The Birth of a Nation* and *Intolerance*, in which the re-creation of ancient Babylon rose 150 feet (46 m) above the East Hollywood bungalows. It didn't matter that *Intolerance*, with its four interwoven stories, was too complex for early audiences; Griffith had single-handedly lifted the form above simple novelty.

By the twenties, resistance to movie companies had softened, and many of the major studios were located in the heart of Hollywood—Columbia, RKO, Paramount, and Warner Brothers were among the movie lots that sprawled beneath the Hollywoodland sign, which was erected to advertise a real estate development in the hills.

These were the heady golden days of the silent era, when Rudolph Valentino and Clara Bow were idolized by millions, despite the fact that they each made only a handful of mediocre pictures. The overall quality of pictures did increase yearly; by the mid-twenties it seemed that moving pictures had nearly reached perfection and there was nothing left for Hollywood to do but turn out beautiful, fluid silent films.

The ability to put sound on film had existed since the earliest days of moving picture technology. Edison had achieved this, as had others. But it never seemed practical or worth the cost to pursue; the big studio bosses saw no need to disturb a good thing.

Jack Warner was the first to take the gamble with sound. He knew that millions of Americans sat riveted to their radios each night and that if movies were to keep the pace, they would have to offer sound. He produced *The Jazz Singer* with

Al Jolson in 1927 and started a revolution that changed the face—and voice—of movies practically overnight. Although some studios held out, hoping the expensive, restrictive talking pictures were a fad, one by one they had to face the music or simply drop out of the competition. Careers of stars who had high-pitched, squeaky voices plummeted while trainloads of actors, writers, and directors from the New York stage arrived daily. William De Mille, Cecil's brother and a director in his own right, summed up the change in Hollywood: "Within two years our little old Hollywood was gone, and in its place stood a fair new city, talking a new language, having different manners and customs; a more terrifying city, full of strange faces, less friendly, more businesslike, twice as populous—and much more cruel."

The talkies were a huge success, despite the fact that the quality of films being shot suffered dramatically. To avoid recording the whir of their mechanisms, cameras were mounted inside stationary soundproof boxes, putting an end to the fluid, exciting movements that had been achieved only shortly before. Actors suddenly appeared stiff, as they were forced to maneuver around hidden microphones in order to be heard. Audiences didn't really seem to care though; they flocked to theatres to view the talking pictures in record numbers.

In 1928 the film industry held the first Academy Awards ceremony, honoring *Wings*, an exciting aerial battle film, with the very first Best Picture award. Hollywood movies entertained people the world over; in fact, American westerns were tremendously popular in Moscow cinemas. Film, as a mass medium, had arrived.

With such mass appeal, censorship is sure to follow. In the movie business, the crackdown came in the form of the Production Code of 1930.

> I can remember vividly how tough it was on actors and actresses when silent pictures gave way to talkies.... There was a fire one day at Paramount, and Clara Bow ran out screaming, "I hope to Christ it was the soundstages!"
>
> —Joseph Mankiewicz

Opposite: A true dream factory, the Warner Brothers studio sprawls across the floor of the San Fernando Valley, surrounded only by horse farms and orchards.
Right: Some consider Mae West's frank sexuality to be chiefly responsible for the restrictive Production Code of 1930.

Basically a list of dos and don'ts regarding language, violence, and sexual matters, the Code was a self-monitoring system started by the major studios to appease outraged religious groups clamoring for decency on the screen. The sexually frank films Mae West made in the mid- to late thirties are often credited for most of the flak the industry fielded at the time.

Still, the studios essentially ignored the Code as soon as it was adopted and continued about their business until 1934. At that time, Catholic laity pressured the industry to obey the Code and put public relations man Joseph Breen in charge of enforcing it. Throughout the thirties and forties, filmmakers bowed to the wishes and whims of the restrictive Breen Office, which actually previewed scripts and suggested changes to bring the pictures back within strict moral bounds. Breen had the industry bending over backward to meet his subjective standards, including absurd restrictions that included "no double beds" and "no kisses longer than eight seconds."

Despite the Code, movies became a national pastime during the Great Depression, as they were often the only form of entertainment families could afford. Movies were a national mania, and events on the screen would often affect the entire country. Marlene Dietrich appeared on film wearing slacks and women across the country took up the fashion. Clark Gable appeared in *It Happened One Night* without an undershirt and sales of the garments plummeted!

America couldn't get enough news from Hollywood. Magazines like *Photoplay* and *Modern Screen* had readerships in the millions, and two women, Louella Parsons and Hedda Hopper, managed to garner a great deal of power by wielding Hollywood gossip columns. These two could launch or topple a career by a simple mention in their columns. Even the biggest stars in Hollywood would stop by Louella's table at lunch to wish her well or send flowers to Hedda on her birthday, knowing that those in their good graces could be assured of good

They made me sound as if I'd been castrated.
—Tallulah Bankhead, on her first sound reproduction

press. The two women were archrivals and used their power to force insiders to grant exclusive scoops, or face the consequences.

The year 1939 was a highwater mark for Hollywood. In that year some of the most memorable pictures in Hollywood history were produced: *The Wizard of Oz, Gunga Din, Mr. Smith Goes to Washington,* and *Gone With the Wind,* to name a few.

Hollywood stood strong through World War II, truly rising to the occasion. The film industry had managed to ignore the world situation, but as soon as the United States entered the war, it was ready to boost the homefront with patriotic war epics and cheap, down and dirty crime stories in the *film noir* genre—the dark texture of which was as much a matter of wartime economics as it was of style.

The war influenced the growth of Hollywood as a city as well. The port of Los Angeles was a major embarkation point for soldiers and sailors heading off to the Pacific. The film community knew a good public relations opportunity when it saw one; in 1942 Bette Davis and John Garfield opened the Hollywood Canteen, a dance hall for servicemen waiting to ship out. Night after night, the men would line up for hours waiting for a chance to get into the Canteen to dance with Joan Crawford or be served a slice of pie by Marlene Dietrich.

During Hollywood's Golden Age, the legendary studio moguls lived their lives like modern-day pharaohs. These were the people who started it all and who now sat at the very top—men like Louis B. Mayer, Harry Cohn, Jack Warner, and Irving Thalberg. Darryl F. Zanuck of Twentieth Century-Fox surrounded himself with Dictaphones at home and at work so that he could instantly record any ideas he might have. The renowned producer David O. Selznick

Below: Hedda Hopper, in one of her trademark hats, schmoozes with Gene Kelly and Jackie Gleason. Opposite: Vivien Leigh as Scarlett O'Hara in producer David O. Selznick's masterful obsession, Gone With the Wind.

We've found a universal language—a power that can make men brothers and end war forever. Remember that. Remember that when you stand in front of a camera!

—D. W. Griffith, to his cast before each picture

demanded that his staff work twenty-four-hour shifts and lorded over a fourteen-writer team for his pride and joy, *Gone With the Wind*. These men controlled the movie-making process from top to bottom, moving directors, stars, and writers around like chess pieces. They dictated new names for the stars, ordered them to change their hair color, or demanded dental work or plastic surgery to alter their facial features. In fact, it was common practice for one studio to loan out a star in its stable to another studio for enormous fees while the loaned-out actor would collect his or her normal and often quite low weekly salary.

In the late forties and early fifties, a series of circumstances tore away at the studios' immense power. First, antitrust legislation enacted in 1948 took away the studios' monopoly on theater ownership, reducing the amount of profit each studio accrued per picture. Next, Hollywood became a target for massive anticommunist attacks. The studio heads, in order to quickly appease conservative Red hunters, blacklisted hundreds of writers, actors, and directors suspected of being communist sympathizers. Working relationships were strained or shattered,

and trust became a thing of the past; it was a dark passage in Hollywood's history that tainted the industry for decades.

Perhaps the biggest challenge to the mighty studios was a little wood and glass box called television. In the early fifties, television cascaded into American homes, carving out a big chunk of the theatrical film audience. The studios fought back by inching into television production, expanding the sheer size of movie screens with systems like CinemaScope, and producing sprawling epics like *Cleopatra and The Ten Commandments* to compete with the fledgling television medium and its smaller format.

The final blow to studio power came as stars finally broke free of the studio system and became free agents, cutting their own deals on a per-picture basis. While the big studios remained somewhat intact, by the sixties they had lost a considerable amount of power. The symbolic headstone for the fabled studio system of the Golden Age could be considered to be the May 1970 auction at the once-proud MGM studios; sold off were Judy Garland's ruby slippers from *The Wizard of Oz*, Tarzan's loincloth, and the chariot Charlton Heston drove in *Ben-Hur*.

[Television is] a twenty-one-inch [52.5-cm] prison. I'm delighted with it because it used to be that films were the lowest form of art. Now we have something to look down on.

— Billy Wilder, director

Their entrepreneurial spirit dwindling, the studios became ripe for takeover by huge corporations hungry for a piece of the Hollywood profits. One by one, through the seventies and early eighties, the eccentric show business moguls were replaced by men in suits with marketing backgrounds and MBAs. The business of running Hollywood became just that, a business, right along with hawking insurance or selling Coca-Cola.

But there was an up side to the situation. As the studios lost power, more control fell into the hands of the filmmakers themselves. Consequently, movies from the late sixties to the present have experienced a creative renaissance.

The turning point is considered by many to be the release of *Easy Rider* in 1969. This low-budget biker flick romanticized the counterculture and made big bucks at the box office. It also paved the way for independent filmmakers to make their mark and created a market for the highly personal, dynamic visions of the *auteurs*—filmmakers like Francis Ford Coppola, Martin

Scorsese, Stanley Kubrick, and Woody Allen—who write, produce, and direct their own pictures, which are then bankrolled and distributed by the big studios.

Today, the word "Hollywood" might be considered more a state of mind than a city in Los Angeles where movies are made. Actually, few movies are made in Hollywood proper (Paramount is the only studio still making movies there), and while Los Angeles is still the hub of American movie-making, many productions are filmed on location. But even this has not dampened the film audience's insatiable desire to know about Hollywood stars—those both before and behind the cameras. The last few years have seen a startling number of new publications and television shows devoted specifically to movies and the people who make them.

Hollywood the city may be run-down, a shadow of what it once was, but the idea of Hollywood—the dream machine—is alive and well. Hollywood remains the teller of stories and the source of them.

Right: The changing face of Hollywood—Jack Nicholson in Easy Rider. *A simple low-budget biker flick, it single-handedly introduced Hollywood to independent film production, antiheroes, and the* auteur *theory in 1969.*

THE HOLLYWOOD SIGN

The famous landmark Hollywood sign was erected high up in the Hollywood Hills in 1923 at a cost of $21,000. When originally built, the sign spelled out "Hollywoodland" in letters thirty feet (9 m) wide and fifty feet (15 m) high, and was studded with thousands of light bulbs. A man living in a small hut behind the sign was employed full-time to change the light bulbs when necessary. The last four letters of the sign fell away in a mudslide during World War II and were never replaced.

The Hollywood sign has been the site of frequent suicide attempts; the first to jump to her death from the sign was failed starlet Peg Entwhistle, who took her first and last leap in 1932.

The dilapidated sign was declared a historic landmark in 1973 and was completely replaced in 1978 at a cost of $27,000 per letter.

CHAPTER TWO

The Stars Are Born

Their faces are universally recognized. They are our idols, our heros, our royalty. The big movie stars who rake in the big bucks for making the biggest films have captivated our emotions and imaginations since the first familiar faces of the earliest flickers. The following chapter takes an in-depth look at how some of Hollywood's leading ladies and leading men reached that coveted pinnacle of popular culture—movie stardom.

Before the star system, the nameless recurring faces in nickelodeons were known only by the companies they worked for ("The Vitagraph Girl") or for the characters they played ("The Waif"). Soon it occurred to studio bosses that once actors had *names*, they would demand more money; later that philosophy flip-flopped as stu-

dios decided it was worth the extra cost to develop stars for publicity reasons.

While many of the earliest stars have faded into obscurity, a few of the greats cast such a spell that their names will remain forever in the register of Hollywood fame.

Lillian Gish, the first leading lady of film, was brought to the screen by D. W. Griffith, who saw her as a paragon of virtue and cast her as a Victorian virgin in many of his biggest pictures. She was hailed as the first modern actress in cinema, for she was able to convey complex emotions on screen without the histrionics of other contemporary actresses. Audiences loved her, and she was paid in kind, being the first woman to earn more than $1 million for acting on film—a sum not to be matched until Elizabeth Taylor was paid

Opposite: D.W. Griffith's paragon of virtue, Lillian Gish, was the first true star of the movies—and the first to earn a million dollars per picture. Above, left to right: Douglas Fairbanks, Mary Pickford, Charlie Chaplin, and D.W. Griffith. These four artists brought together their wealth and power to produce their own films—and keep most of the profits—as United Artists.

a cool million for her performance in *Cleopatra* in 1960. (Even then Gish still had Taylor beat; she received her fortune for appearing in three short features, adding up to less than half the screen time of *Cleopatra*!) By 1925, Gish was being paid a whopping $8,000 a week under contract with MGM. Only a few years later, after many fine pictures, she fell from favor with studio publicists, who considered her overpaid and out of fashion. She moved on to a distinguished career in the theater, although she occasionally appeared on film and television.

Charlie Chaplin's Little Tramp character assured him an eternal place in the history of stardom. Chaplin's star was launched by the masses of urban immigrants struggling to make a go of it in America. They identified with the little man with the funny mustache, a constant underdog who managed to stay one step ahead of fate.

Chaplin was the son of a London vaudeville couple. His father died of alcohol abuse at the age of thirty-seven, and his mother went insane from malnutrition while he was still a young man. It's easy to see that Chaplin became a performer and perfected his craft not so much for the sake of art, but as a means of survival. Early film audiences empathized with his pain and suffering in the characterization of the Little Tramp and made Charlie Chaplin a star.

During his long career, Chaplin was both hailed as a genius and mocked as the subject of scandal and public scorn (see page 138), but he remained true to his artistic and personal vision and fought off bitterness. While accepting an honorary Oscar in 1972, he wept, managing only to say, "Beautiful people."

Mary Pickford, another silent screen idol, became a multimillionairess by the time she was twenty-seven, through her ability to tug America's heartstrings in roles like Cinderella and Pollyanna. "Little Mary" married swashbuckler Douglas Fairbanks, several times her costar and a huge star in his own right. Together they were the king and

I've made a career, in a sense, of playing sons of bitches.
— Kirk Douglas

Above: Greta Garbo and John Gilbert in the incredibly romantic— even erotic—1927 silent film Flesh and the Devil.

queen of Hollywood in the twenties. They were known the world over (on a visit to Moscow over a million fans gathered to greet them) and became so wealthy and powerful they were able to found United Artists—with Chaplin and D. W. Griffith—to produce their own pictures and keep a bigger percentage of the huge profits for themselves. They held legendary dinner parties in their Hollywood home, the famed "Pickfair," where on any given night Albert Einstein might demonstrate relativity at the table or Winston Churchill might discuss world affairs. In a very short time, Hollywood's movie stars had become, in effect, America's aristocracy.

With the talkies entered a sweeping new range of stars, personalities with the skill to rifle off the rapid-fire dialogue that writers crammed into every picture.

The first true star of the talkies was undoubtedly Greta Garbo, who came to America as the protégée of Swedish director Mauritz Stall as a condition of his contract with MGM. The forcefully erotic silent pictures she made, like *Flesh and*

the Devil and *A Woman of Affairs*, made Garbo a star, but her Hollywood stature increased even more dramatically when she finally spoke in 1930's *Anna Christie.*

MGM at first did not know how to handle Garbo, trying in vain to wedge her into the usual stereotypical female star personas. Baffled by her reluctance to conform, the studio eventually turned it to advantage by promoting her as a mysterious recluse. The image stuck and grew to legendary proportions, echoed in the famous line, "I want to be alone." According to biographer John Bainbridge, Garbo claimed she never said that line, explaining, "I only said, 'I want to be left alone.' There is all the difference."

After a successful string of films—which now seem to be little more than frames for her alluring alabaster features—Garbo left Hollywood for a temporary retirement in 1942—a retirement which eventually became permanent.

Why? Theories abound: perhaps she was concerned that the war in Europe would disrupt her largest market, or perhaps she had grown

Producers don't make stars. God makes stars, and the public recognizes His handiwork.

—Samuel Goldwyn

tired of constant squabbles with her bosses at MGM. No one really knows for sure. When she died in 1990, she took her secrets with her.

Garbo was the first of an avalanche of enduring stars the thirties would bring, including a man they called "The King" twenty-five years before Elvis swiveled into fame—Clark Gable.

Gable, convinced that his fame would be fleeting, remarked that he wasn't buying anything that he "couldn't fit on the Chief"—the train back East. He had reason to be wary; his star didn't rise overnight. When he tested for Warner Brothers, he was rejected by Darryl F. Zanuck, who snapped: "His ears are too big. He looks like an ape." But Depression Era audiences wanted just that—a hulking, outspoken, working man's hero. By the time David O. Selznick was casting *Gone With the Wind*, Gable was the only man he would have play Rhett Butler, no matter how high the cost. Gable was the consummate movie star from the time he appeared in *Dance, Fools, Dance* with Joan Crawford in 1931 (a year in which he made *eleven* movies) until he died in 1960.

Gable didn't reign as king alone. He had a queen—his wife, another great star of the day, Carole Lombard. Carole Lombard seemed to be the perfect match for Gable. She lived just as vividly off the screen as on. A talented comedienne in her films, she was also a ribald practical joker with a flair for swearing offscreen. And she was said to have been as much a sizzling, tempestuous lover in real life as she appeared to millions on film.

In classic bawdy style, Lombard first met Gable at a party. She made her grand entrance by arriving in the back of an ambulance and being carried through the door on a stretcher. She grabbed Gable's attention and held it for the rest of her life. Some say their marriage was a publicity venture, cooked up by studio public relations people, but it is well known that the two loved each other dearly; Gable and Lombard were Hollywood's most glamorous couple of the thirties (see page 78).

Perhaps the ultimate star story from Hollywood's golden days is that of Joan

Crawford, hailed as one of the biggest stars of the early talkies and still beloved by fans when she finished her career fifty years later. Through it all, she flowed from one persona to the next, hanging onto stardom for dear life—from Jazz Baby of the roaring twenties to Glamour Queen for MGM in the late thirties. Pulling through a slump in the mid-forties that would have driven any other star under, she bounced back to a fresh postwar career that culminated in the cutting-edge madness of *Whatever Happened to Baby Jane?*

At her lowest point, before her 1945 comeback in *Mildred Pierce*, American exhibitors had labeled Crawford "box-office poison"; MGM came

Above: This sedate, waiflike early portrait of Carole Lombard belies her reputation as a witty wild woman who took pleasure in swearing and pulling practical jokes.

This King stuff is pure bull. I eat and drink and go to the bathroom just like anybody else. I'm just a lucky slob who happened to be in the right place at the right time.

— Clark Gable

The name's got to go.
— Harry Cohn, to Jack Lemmon

to her defense, revealing that she had received an incredible nine hundred thousand fan letters. Crawford went on to make movies for another thirty-five years.

While Joan Crawford continuously changed her approach to keep her name in lights, tough-as-nails Bette Davis remained fiercely independent through it all to become the top screen actress of her day. By 1935 she had proven herself, having won an Oscar for her performance in *Dangerous*. By then she knew she was worth more than a cheap retread of Dashiell Hammett's *The Maltese Falcon*, titled *Satan Met a Lady*, which was scheduled to be her next project at

Warner Brothers. (The first film version, in 1931, was called *Dangerous Female*.) The studio refused to put her in a better picture, so Davis packed her bags and set off for England, intending to put an end to her feud with the studio and to make a picture out of contract.

Consequently, Warners sued Davis, and the court ruled in the studio's favor—after all, Davis was contracted to the studio for another five years. But the victory for Warners was a hollow one. Unbeknownst to her, Davis' good friend, distinguished actor George Arliss, spoke with Jack Warner on her behalf and convinced the mogul that prestigious films and stars could actually

make him money. Warner pledged to treat Davis to better roles upon her return. Davis received true star treatment until she was released from her contract in 1949.

Even then, when insiders felt her career was over, the grand dame of the screen came back in *All About Eve* as Margo Channing, a role no one but Davis could have played to such perfection and for which she won another Oscar.

Katharine Hepburn, another staunchly independent woman, also rose to stardom in the thirties and fought long and hard to stay there. Hollywood didn't quite know how to react when she turned her earliest starring roles for RKO into hits in the early thirties. She displayed disdain for Hollywood etiquette, establishing herself as an outsider. After a couple of good films that she made failed to earn money, RKO dropped her. She returned to Broadway, where she starred in and acquired the movie rights to *The Philadelphia Story*. In 1940, she was back in Hollywood with an Oscar nomination for her role in the film and a new studio contract, her star shining more brightly than ever. Not long after that, MGM first paired her with Spencer Tracy in *Woman of the Year*, and the sparks flew immediately.

Spencer Tracy discovered his penchant for acting while in college. Hearing that his school's debate team was heading to New York on a tour, Tracy joined up; while in New York, he snuck away to audition for the American Academy of Dramatic Arts. Frank Havens Sargent, founder of the Academy, found Tracy a refreshing, manly change from the "effeminate or too pretty actors...flocking into the theatre." Tracy promptly dropped out of school and remained in New York to act.

The huge success of his Broadway performance in *The Last Mile* brought him out to Hollywood, and there he began what Stanley Kramer (who later directed Tracy in *Inherit the Wind*) has called "a one-man rebellion." Largely kept a secret from his adoring public, Tracy's lifelong bout with alcoholism tried the patience of all who worked with and loved him. Fox signed him first but found him too difficult. When Fox let his

contract lapse, Irving Thalberg wanted to bring him over to MGM, a suggestion to which Louis B. Mayer responded, "We already got one drunken son of a bitch to contend with—Wallace Beery—

Opposite: Katharine Hepburn and James Stewart in **The Philadelphia Story.** *Right: Spencer Tracy and Jean Harlow in* **Goldie.**

DISCOVERED!

Ida Lupino tagged along with her mother, actress Connie Emerald, to an audition for *Her First Affair* in 1933. Emerald was turned down for being too old for the role of a provocative teenager, and Lupino, then fifteen, was given the part instead.

Alan Dawn spotted a young girl playing in a neighbor's yard while visiting friends. At the time, he was looking for a lively tomboy for the film *A Perfect Crime*. He cast the young Carole Lombard on the spot.

George Raft was a petty mobster sent to extort money out of night-club queen Texas Guinan. Instead, he accepted her offer to act in her autobiographical film *Queen of the Night Clubs*. He played only the "tough guy" in movie roles from that day on.

Fatty Arbuckle, a plumber's assistant, was sent to unclog comedy producer Mack Sennett's drain in 1913. Sennett immediately offered the portly boy a job in his Keystone Kops comedies.

Rock Hudson was a mailman lucky enough to have talent agent Henry Willson on his route. Willson arranged for Hudson to meet director Raoul Walsh, for whom he made his screen debut.

Ellen Burstyn was given her first major screen role in *Tropic of Cancer* after the director heard her deliver a political speech.

Opposite: Cary Grant began his career as a clown on the Coney Island boardwalk, but ultimately became the epitome of the sophisticated leading man in Hollywood in the 1940s.

who needs another?" But Thalberg was successful at persuading Mayer, and eighteen MGM pictures later, Tracy was paired with Hepburn.

Tracy and Hepburn went on to wage the battle of the sexes in a succession of films like *Adam's Rib* and *Woman of the Year*, all the while maintaining a lifelong relationship. She and Tracy came out of retirement together in 1967 to make *Guess Who's Coming to Dinner?* This was Tracy's last film. Hepburn won an Oscar for her role in the movie and went on to win two more for *The Lion in Winter* and *On Golden Pond*.

One of the more distinctive voices crackling out of early cinema speakers belonged to Cary Grant. Grant, born Archie Leach in Bristol, England, started his career as a clown on New York's Coney Island boardwalk. His first screen test, for Paramount's Astoria, Long Island, studio, was a bust. Let down gently, he was told, "You're bowlegged, and your neck is too thick."

Still, he persisted. He moved out to Hollywood but fared no better there until he was asked to play opposite director Marion Gering's wife in her screen test at Paramount. Archie agreed to do the test, only to be slightly embarrassed when he was given a contract and Mrs. Gering was not.

Paramount had one request: lose the name. Actress Fay Wray suggested the first name Cary. He chose Grant from Paramount's master list of available and approved names. The new Cary Grant went on to become one of the true kings of light comedy in the thirties and forties in films like *Bringing Up Baby* and *Arsenic and Old Lace*.

If Cary Grant epitomized the sophisticated leading man in the 1940s, it was John Wayne who stood for the macho ideal, the man's man, in films of the day. Wayne began his film career as a summer job and made his first appearance in film under his real name, Marion Morrison.

John Wayne's father was a druggist who moved his family to Los Angeles in 1912 to try his hand at farming. He soon realized that farming didn't suit him; he moved the family once again, this time to Glendale, a nearby suburb, and returned to his career as a druggist. Marion was five when the family settled in Glendale and took to roaming the area with his dog, Duke. The boy and his dog became well known to local firemen, who remembered the dog's name more easily than the boy's. Before long, Marion and his dog were both known as Duke. The name stuck with Wayne for the rest of his life.

Marion Morrison was quite an athlete and attended the University of Southern California on a football scholarship. The year was 1926, the heady days of silent films. At the time, world-renowned cowboy star Tom Mix was a great football fan. Mix managed to get coveted U.S.C. football tickets by offering players summer jobs at Fox studios in return for good seats at the games. One such player was Morrison, who moved set pieces and filled in as stuntman on many now-forgotten silent westerns. It was on a studio lot that the macho action director, Raoul Walsh, spotted Morrison and cast him as the lead in his 1930 B western, *The Big Trail*. And it was for that film that Walsh created his young star's name: John Wayne.

I have decided that while I'm a star I will be every inch and every moment a star. Everyone from the studio gateman to the highest executive will know it.

— Gloria Swanson

You make a star,
you make a
monster.

—Sam Spiegel,
producer who
cast unknown
Peter O'Toole
as Lawrence
of Arabia

Wayne's career climbed slowly until the legendary American director John Ford took a chance on the B-movie hunk and cast him as the lead in his 1939 classic western, *Stagecoach*. The film made Wayne a consummate star, one whose career continued to grow to legendary proportions.

By 1967, *Time* magazine declared Wayne "the greatest money-maker in movie history," thanks in large part to the western films he'd made with Ford and others during the 1940s, films such as *She Wore a Yellow Ribbon*, *Red River*, and *Fort Apache*. Between 1949 and 1972, there was only one year, 1958, when Wayne's name did not appear on a list of the top ten box-office hits in America.

In 1964, Wayne, whose likeness had graced cigarette advertisements for years and who was known to smoke four packs of cigarettes a day, was diagnosed with lung cancer. Half of one of his lungs was removed, but still he continued to work hard and went on to win an Oscar for his performance in *True Grit* in 1969. He continued to make films for years afterward, commanding the respect and admiration of his fans until his death ten years later.

When Hollywood was rocked by the communist scandals of the late forties and the coming of television, the industry tried to compensate for its loss by offering more of everything—vulgarity and sensitivity, youthfulness and safety, color and excitement, and at the same time, more maturity—creating in the fifties a cinema of contradictions. A new breed of actors became stars, many of whom came from the ranks of New York's The Actors Studio, trained in "The Method."

The most talented, brash, and controversial of these Method actors was Marlon Brando. Brando went to New York at nineteen, feeling a failure at playing the drums, at school, and at athletics. He found his calling at The Actors Studio. Only four years after his arrival in New York, his successes on Broadway brought him to the attention of Hollywood, which by 1946 was hungry for him to screen-test. He was supremely uninterested and demonstrated his feelings during a screen test for Twentieth Century-Fox by playing with a yo-yo.

It wasn't until Elia Kazan brought the Broadway smash *A Streetcar Named Desire* to film in 1951 that Brando became a film star (it was only his second film after *The Men*). But he continued to scorn the Hollywood community, dressing in jeans and dirty T-shirts wherever he went, choosing to live in New York and crash at the home of his agent, Jay Kanter, whenever he was in town. The agent had to loan Brando a suit whenever they went out for dinner—Brando didn't own one. Finally, Kanter asked Brando to buy a couple of suits. Brando consented, buying three used suits out of Kanter's closet; he didn't want to have to break in any new ones!

Hollywood may have detested the slovenly Method actor, but audiences identified with Brando; his dark side infused his characters in *The Wild One* and *On the Waterfront* with a riveting sense of danger, propelling him to cult status with fifties youths.

Another fifties Method actor lived fast, died young, and left a cult of personality that still thrives today.

James Dean was a lonesome child. His mother died when he was nine and Dean's father, worried he could not give the boy a proper upbringing, sent him to live with his aunt and uncle in Illinois. Dean was able to channel his pain

Left: Marion Morrison appeared on the big screen for the first time under his new name, John Wayne, in the early talkie western The Big Trail. *Although this was his first starring role, Wayne exhibited plenty of the easygoing charm that would make him a giant star. Opposite: Marlon Brando played a tough misfit longshoreman in the 1954 smash* On the Waterfront. *Brando infused his characters with a sense of danger, appealing to young audiences in the very conservative Eisenhower era.*

and loneliness into competitive situations in high school—he once ranked near the top of a speech competition in which he snapped the judges to attention by screaming before launching into a tormented reading of Dickens' *The Madman*. After high school, Dean went to Los Angeles to live with his father and began acting in a halfhearted way, managing to land a Coca-Cola commercial while studying at the University of California at Los Angeles.

While in Los Angeles, Dean was convinced by a friend that New York was the place to study acting. Dean moved there and studied the Method with the Strasbergs. His work in New York led to a string of successful appearances on early television—where he angered other cast members with his mumbling attempts at capturing real-life speech. He was cast in several Broadway plays and won a Tony award for playing Bachir, a homosexual Arab houseboy, in the hit play *The Immoralist*. The part brought Dean to the attention of Elia Kazan, who cast him as the errant son in *East of Eden*. When *East of Eden* was released, people began paying attention to Dean, but with only a fraction of the intensity that was to come.

After *East of Eden*, Dean quickly went into production on two more movies, *Rebel Without a Cause* in the winter of 1955 and *Giant* the following summer and autumn. In the meantime, he was busy with his latest hobby, auto racing (after chess, bongo drums, poetry, etc.); he had even won a few local races. The studio, familiar with Dean's latest fascination, forbade him to race until photography on *Giant* was completed. Eager to get behind the wheel, Dean scheduled to compete in a race in Salinas, California, the weekend after the final scenes had been shot. He set out for Salinas on Friday, September 30, 1955, in his brand new Porsche Spyder that he had named "Little Bastard," accompanied by his mechanic, Rolf Wutherich.

At 3:30 P.M., Dean was pulled over for speeding just outside Bakersfield. Two hours later, as twilight was approaching, Wutherich was getting sleepy from the drone of the engine. Suddenly he was roused from sleep by Dean

The Cast

> If [James Dean] had lived, they'd have discovered he wasn't a legend.
>
> — Humphrey Bogart

Opposite: The ultimate cult figure of American cinema—James Dean in Rebel Without a Cause. Above: Elizabeth Taylor as Cleopatra—her ultimate "rich bitch" role.

shouting, "That guy up there's gotta stop; he'll see us." They were Dean's last words. He was killed instantly as the two cars collided. Wutherich was thrown clear and miraculously survived; somehow the driver of the other car walked away with a bruised nose.

A month after the crash, *Rebel* opened with its ironic scene in which Dean survives a race with death. That irony, plus his startling performance, galvanized the lost generation of youth in America, and to this day Dean's image as a reckless rebel without a cause is still as potent to the young as it was in 1955.

Perhaps the most enduring star of postwar Hollywood is Elizabeth Taylor. The daughter of an archetypal stage mother, Sarah Taylor, Elizabeth was groomed to be a star from the moment she signed her contract with MGM in 1942 at the age of ten. Her mother accompanied her to the studio every day, drilling her on how to hit her mark and work within the nimbus of her key light. When Elizabeth was cast as the twelve-year-old heroine of *National Velvet* in 1944, her mother turned her room into a horsey boudoir of bridles, saddles, and statues; Elizabeth even took to referring to herself as Velvet.

WHAT'S IN A NAME?

Lucille le Sueur's name was deemed "too difficult to pronounce" and "too French" by her studio, which cooked up a national fan magazine contest to help rename their star and offered a $500 prize for the chosen entry. The money was eventually sent to the person who suggested "Joan Crawford."

Jane Peters became Carol Lombard by borrowing the last name of close family friends. A misspelled promotional poster for *Safety in Numbers* listed the actress as Carole Lombard. "What the hell," she said, "let's keep it that way."

Here is a list of the names some Hollywood stars were born with:

Eddie Albert
   Edward Albert Heimberger
Woody Allen
   Allen Stewart Konigsberg
Eve Arden
   Eunice Quedens
Brigitte Bardot
   Camille Javal
Orson Bean
   Dallas Frederick Burrows

WHAT'S IN A NAME? (continued)

Jack Benny
Benjamin Kubelsky

Charles Bronson
Charles Buchinsky

Albert Brooks
Albert Einstein

Mel Brooks
Melvin Kaminsky

Ellen Burstyn
Edna Gillooly

Richard Burton
Richard Jenkins, Jr.

Red Buttons
Aaron Chwatt

Michael Caine
Maurice Micklewhite, Jr.

Cyd Charisse
Tula Finklea

Lee J. Cobb
Leo Jacoby

Claudette Colbert
Lili Claudette Chauchoin

Gary Cooper
Frank Cooper

Tony Curtis
Bernard Schwartz

Sandra Dee
Alexandra Zuck

Yvonne De Carlo
Peggy Yvonne Middleton

Phyllis Diller
Phyllis Driver

Kirk Douglas
Issur Danielovitch

Douglas Fairbanks
Douglas Elton Ullman

After the film's huge success, MGM brought Sarah Taylor onto the payroll, paying the young star's mother $10,000 a year to be her child's guardian.

Elizabeth grew quickly into a young woman (some feel she was forced along) and was hailed by family friend Hedda Hopper as "the most beautiful girl in the world." She began the first of a long line of "rich bitch" roles opposite Montgomery Clift in *A Place in the Sun*, and over time, honed the act to precision. Later, her many romances and marriages became the stuff of legend; still, she emerged as practically the only classic movie star to weather the turbulent fifties and sixties with her glamorous image intact, pushing herself to create memorable screen roles in *Cat on a Hot Tin Roof*, *Who's Afraid of Virginia Woolf?*, and others.

One of the biggest stars in Hollywood today not only rode out those turbulent decades, but used them to his advantage, to become one of the more offbeat talents in movies. Perhaps it's not surprising that Jack Nicholson has such a captivating, on-the-edge quality about his work. He was born to seventeen-year-old June Nicholson but was raised by his grandparents. He was told they were his parents and that his mother was his sister—until her death in 1975. He never knew his real father.

Nicholson's career began when he went to work for Roger Corman—king of the B pictures—who cranked out low-budget movies in the fifties and sixties that were targeted to teens at drive-in theaters. He appeared in Corman's 1958 B film *Cry Baby Killer* and for the next ten years continued to act, write, and direct for Corman. Nicholson's big break came in 1969 when he signed on to play George Hanson in Dennis Hopper's *Easy Rider*. No one involved in this low-budget, independently produced biker movie had any idea how much money it would make or how important it would turn out be; the film single-handedly shook Hollywood out of its post-television doldrums, ushered in the antihero, and signaled the arrival of the counterculture to the mainstream. It also made Nicholson a star who earned millions

injecting his edgy personality into films like *Chinatown*, *The Shining*, *Terms of Endearment*, and *Batman*.

Another star who came out of the sixties specializing in the antihero character is Dustin Hoffman, a man who has achieved the reputation of being the classic difficult-to-work-with actor. He began cultivating this reputation early; on stage in the seventh grade as Tiny Tim in *A*

Below: Part of Jack Nicholson's star appeal is that he has never truly lost his B-movie edge; he stars in prestige productions, yet appeals to our prurient interests.

Above: The classic handsome leading man, Robert Redford stumbled into stardom practically by accident. In 1990 he played a suave American gambler in Havana, another link in a long chain of good-guy roles.

Hoffman's success on stage in New York led the producers of *The Graduate* to take a chance. They cast the thirty-year-old Hoffman as the recent college graduate, Benjamin Braddock. The movie was a tremendous success, and once again, Hoffman was seen by the youth audience as someone they could identify with. The realism with which Hoffman plays his characters in films such as *Midnight Cowboy*, *Tootsie*, and *Rain Man* has endeared him to an entire generation of fans.

The consummate movie star of the late sixties and early seventies, one who bundles together talent and looks with social consciousness, is Robert Redford.

The young Redford wanted to be a professional baseball player—he considered actors "sissies" in his youth—and actually backed into his career as film superstar. After trying baseball in college, he became discouraged and traveled around Europe, eventually studying art in Florence. When that didn't pan out, he came back to America and began studying art in New York City. He developed an interest in set design and—in order to gain a "better understanding" of the theater—began taking acting classes. Almost reluctantly, he accepted roles on television and stage—and on the big screen. In 1967, Redford suddenly found himself cast with Jane Fonda in a big-time Hollywood film, Neil Simon's *Barefoot in the Park*. In his very next picture he costarred with Paul Newman in *Butch Cassidy and the Sundance Kid*, which turned the reluctant Redford into a bona fide box-office star.

Off screen, he has been somewhat outspoken about his political views, mostly concerning the environment and equal rights. But critics cite his long list of safe films that don't push the limits of common liberal viewpoints as a failure of Redford as an artist. Frequently threatening to retire from acting, Redford has used his ranch in Utah as a base for the Sundance Institute, a nonprofit workshop for aspiring new filmmakers.

While these stars are often seen at gala Hollywood events or on talk shows plugging their latest films, one well-trained actor, who brings an

Christmas Carol, the young Hoffman had been tricked into altering his last line, and he boldly closed the show with, "God bless us all, God damn it!"

Hoffman says that he stuck with acting in the beginning "to meet girls." Apparently he wasn't sure he could do it any other way, for he spent years in therapy coming to grips with his five-foot-six-inch (168-cm) stature. Acting, in the end, was the answer. He came out of his shell at The Actors Studio in New York City, where he roomed with Gene Hackman and Robert Duvall, becoming a notorious ladies' man.

WHAT'S IN A NAME? (continued)

W. C. Fields
William Claude Duckenfield

Greta Garbo
Greta Louisa Gustafsson

Judy Garland
Frances Gumm

Paulette Goddard
Marion Levy

Jean Harlow
Harlean Carpenter

Susan Hayward
Edythe Marrener

Barbara Hershey
Barbara Herzstein

William Holden
William Franklin Beedle, Jr.

Boris Karloff
William Henry Pratt

Veronica Lake
Constance Ockleman

Hedy Lamarr
Hedwig Kiesler

Janet Leigh
Jeanette Helen Morrison

Jerry Lewis
Joseph Levitch

Myrna Loy
Myrna Williams

Bela Lugosi
Bela Ferenc Dezco

Karl Malden
Mladen Sekulovich

Jayne Mansfield
Vera Jane Palmer

Dean Martin
Dino Paul Crocetti

I don't want to be an old-fash-ioned movie star in the true sense of that term. A Hollywood "star" is death as far as real acting is concerned.

— Robert De Niro

Here are just two of the many faces of Robert De Niro. Opposite: As the swaggering boxer Jake La Motta in Raging Bull. *Right: As the twisted stand-up comedian Rupert Pupkin in* The King of Comedy.

incredible amount of truth and power to his roles, chooses instead to let his work speak almost entirely for itself. Although he has become somewhat more accessible as he has matured, Robert De Niro is renowned for being almost impossible to interview. He is a secretive man who at one time did not divulge his home telephone number even to his close friends, forcing them to make appointments with his assistants just to see him.

De Niro was born in New York City's Greenwich Village in 1943. The son of bohemian artists who divorced when he was two, he was raised by his mother in the city, and dropped out of school at sixteen to study acting with Stella Adler, the woman responsible for teaching Brando his craft. De Niro managed to land a string of unmemorable screen roles, but eventually caught the eye of director (and childhood acquaintance) Martin Scorsese, who cast him in his feature *Mean Streets*. The young De Niro stole the picture and that same year, 1973, played his breakthrough role as a terminally ill baseball player in *Bang the Drum Slowly*. The next year he played the young Vito Corleone in Francis Ford Coppola's *The Godfather, Part II* — a younger counterpart to Brando's 1972 Academy Award–winning role. De Niro, too, won an Academy Award for his portrayal. The young actor had arrived as the latest master of his craft.

Six years later, in 1980, De Niro won his second Oscar for his portrayal of boxer Jake La Motta in Scorsese's *Raging Bull*. Perhaps no actor has worked harder for a role; De Niro gained an extra fifty pounds (22.7 kg) for scenes that portrayed La Motta's middle-age decline. But De Niro puts this kind of effort into each role he plays; he perfected a specific Sicilian dialect for *The Godfather, Part II*, and for his role as Travis Bickle in *Taxi Driver* he actually got a hacker's license and drove a cab in New York City. The dedication and effort have paid off; in a string of fine films, including *The King of Comedy*, *Midnight Run*, *Awakenings*, and *Goodfellas*, De Niro has brought his powerful characters startlingly to life.

Continuing his pursuit of non-Hollywood success, he has invested in the Tribeca Film Center in New York City, where he envisions bold, independent film companies and directors using the production offices and screening rooms. It is De Niro's hope that the center will foster more creative filmmaking.

Of course, the well-trained actors who rose to stardom in the sixties and seventies weren't all men. Meryl Streep, one of today's biggest film actresses, was trained and highly honored at the Yale School of Drama. She also achieved great critical acclaim for her quality work in Joseph Papp's New York Shakespeare Festival. She is a shining example of the most recent breed of American star: professional, earnest, independent, and allowed to live a quiet private life out of the Hollywood spotlight.

Indeed, Streep takes her privacy very seriously, even wearing a wig and dark glasses to go to the grocery store near her Upper East Side New York City home. Since Meryl Streep began creating her highly complex characters on the screen, as she did in *Julia*, *Sophie's Choice*, and

WHAT'S IN A NAME? (continued)

Walter Matthau
Walter Matuschanskvasky

Ray Milland
Reginald Truscott-Jones

Marilyn Monroe
Norma Jeane Mortensen

Yves Montand
Ivo Levi

Robert Montgomery
Henry Montgomery

Slim Pickens
Louis Lindley

Stefanie Powers
Stephanie Federkewicz

Edward G. Robinson
Emmanuel Goldenberg

Ginger Rogers
Virginia McMath

Mickey Rooney
Joe Yule, Jr.

Susan Sarandon
Susan Tomaling

Martin Sheen
Ramon Esteves

Barbara Stanwyck
Ruby Stevens

Robert Taylor
Spangler Arlington Brugh

John Wayne
Marion Michael Morrison

Gene Wilder
Gerald Silberman

Natalie Wood
Natasha Gurdin

Gig Young
Byron Elsworth Barr

Above: Meryl Streep has made a career of playing extremely complex characters, as in The French Lieutenant's Woman. *Opposite: Jessica Lange as the tortured actress Frances Farmer, in the acclaimed* Frances.

dropping out of school in Minnesota to study mime in Paris, Lange returned to New York where she painted, acted now and then, and modeled for catalogs. Her big break—which started and nearly ended her career—was being cast in Dino De Laurentiis' remake of *King Kong* in 1976. She signed a seven-year contract with the producer, who immediately went about creating a myth around his mechanical ape's leading lady, building her up as a gorgeous cover-girl-turned-actress (which she thoroughly resented). The film was a critical and financial flop. Typecast as a silly blonde who screamed well, Lange saw her career languish for years after the film's release.

Nevertheless, she was cast in a few inconsequential films and even played opposite Jack Nicholson in a remake of *The Postman Always Rings Twice* (which was also heavily panned). Her big triumph came in 1982, the year in which she gave two fabulous performances: as the mentally tortured Frances Farmer in the biographical film *Frances* and opposite Dustin Hoffman in the incredible box-office and critical smash *Tootsie*.

Lange finally had proved herself to audiences and to Hollywood. Shortly after these two acclaimed performances, she was competing for top female roles with Meryl Streep herself. Lange, too, shuns the Hollywood scene, spending her free time with playwright and actor Sam Shepard and their children on their farm in Virginia.

It has been said that Tom Cruise is a star because guys want to be like him and girls want to be with him. Perhaps most of those guys and girls don't realize that Cruise was set to become a priest and that he was actually enrolled at a Franciscan seminary in Cincinnati, Ohio. He eventually left the seminary, saying he just "loved women too much to give *that* up."

Cruise discovered that he had a knack for acting and took off for New York, where those who knew him claim Cruise was a very different guy—a muscle-bound greaser. Perhaps that helped him land a role in *The Outsiders*, a film about gangs in the sixties, where he met Emilio Estevez, Matt Dillon, and Rob Lowe—all members of what became known as "The Brat Pack."

The French Lieutenant's Woman, times have changed; stars are no longer required to conform to a particular type and play it forever. Today's stars are more like chameleons than at any time in history and the stereotyped casting associated with old Hollywood is now more prevalent in work on television.

Jessica Lange fought against the last vestiges of the old typecasting mentality during the frustrating first phase of her rise to fame. After

I was like a kept woman during my twenty-one years at MGM. Hollywood was like an expensive, beautifully run club. You didn't need to carry money. Your face was your credit card.

—Walter Pidgeon

The Stars Are Born

Despite the tremendous success of movies such as *Risky Business* and *Rain Man*, critics put down Cruise as a mere pretty boy. But he devotes himself thoroughly to each acting project, virtually becoming the character he plays. For example, he spent a lot of time hanging around the U.S. Navy's elite Blue Angels before shooting *Top Gun* in 1986. It seems to have paid off; audiences couldn't get enough of that film and, since then, Tom Cruise has been one of the very brightest stars in Hollywood, boasting millions of fans and earning millions per picture.

Star power is resilient—when you've got it, you've got it. A classic example of a star whose brilliance only increases is Jodie Foster.

Foster was born and raised in Los Angeles and was acting by the time she was three, appearing in Coppertone commercials. Before long she graduated to television situation comedies and Disney films; as a child actress, she eventually became the primary breadwinner for her family—including her manager mother, a sister, and two brothers—after her father abandoned them.

Foster burst onto the big screen as the teenage prostitute in Martin Scorsese's *Taxi*

Left: Zipped up and ready to fly in the 1986 hit **Top Gun**, *Tom Cruise became one of Hollywood's hottest male stars. Above: Jodie Foster in* **The Accused**, *a role that won her an Academy Award for Best Actress. A true modern star, she possesses beauty, brains, and the courage to play complex, controversial roles.*

Driver—a role that landed her an Academy Award nomination. The talented young actress seemed destined for stardom. Unfortunately, her performance caught more than the attention of the Academy at the time. Somewhere out in a darkened movie house sat a troubled young man, John Hinckley. The violence-drenched urban nightmare Scorsese brought to the screen affected Hinckley deeply; he paid to see the film scores of times. He identified with the hero, taxi driver Travis Bickle, and he fell in some sort of demented love with Foster. Eventually, his unrequited love drove him to a twisted attempt to impress her: in 1981, he fired six shots at President Ronald Reagan, wounding him and several others.

With the question "Why me?" running through her mind, Foster retreated into academia, majoring in literature at Yale. She continued to act in films, using her hefty salary to put herself through school.

While the rest of the world dwelled on her past and the Hinckley connection, Foster rose above it all and was somehow able to put the horrendous situation out of her mind and concentrate on her work. By 1988, in the disturbing film *The Accused*, it was obvious that Jodie Foster was in complete control of herself and her craft. She won an Academy Award for Best Actress in her role as a gang-rape survivor with a questionable past. The film seemed to act as a crucible, and fans finally looked at Foster in a new light. As the strong female protagonist in 1991's release, *Silence of the Lambs*, Foster finally claimed her rightful spot as one of our most intelligent actresses and brightest stars. (She has also directed her first film, *Little Man Tate*, released in late 1991.)

The world has changed a lot since the early silent days, and Hollywood is barely recognizable. But the movie stars still shine, and we, the audience, continue to gaze.

WHATEVER BECAME OF THOSE CHILD STARS?

NAME	CHILD STAR OF...	GREW UP TO BECOME...
Freddie Bartholomew	*David Copperfield, Little Lord Fauntleroy*	New York advertising executive
Robert Blake	*Our Gang* comedies	Tough-guy star of *In Cold Blood* and TV's *Baretta*
Jackie Coogan	Starred in *The Kid* with Charlie Chaplin	Ended up as Uncle Fester on TV's *The Addams Family*
Jackie Cooper	Oscar-nominated role, *Skippy* (1931), *Our Gang* comedies	B-movie and TV actor/director, "guest star"
Bobby Driscoll	Disney's *Song of the South*, Oscar winner for *The Window* (1949)	Heroin addict, died a vagrant and was buried in a pauper's grave, New York, 1968
Mark Lester	*Oliver!* (1961)	Adult actor trying to play children in films like *Dance Under the Elms* and *Jungle Boy*
Roddy McDowell	*How Green Was My Valley, Lassie Come-Home*	Successful adult actor, *The Poseidon Adventure, Planet of the Apes*, etc.
Hayley Mills	*The Parent Trap, Pollyanna, That Darn Cat!*	Nineteen-year-old lover, then wife, of fifty-one-year-old director Roy Boulting
Mickey Rooney	The Andy Hardy film series, *Boys' Town, Babes in Arms*	Eight-time husband, screen host of *That's Entertainment*, star of *Sugar Babies* on Broadway
Carl "Alfalfa" Switzer	*Our Gang* comedies	Shooting victim in an argument over $50.00, 1959
Shirley Temple	*Stand Up and Cheer, The Little Colonel*	U.S. Representative to the United Nations, ambassador to Czechoslovakia

CHAPTER THREE
Sex Symbols

Hollywood has always offered the world more than the usual excitement, thrills, and romance—more than dashing leading ladies and leading men. Hollywood both dictates and reflects trends in our culture with its symbols of feminine and masculine ideals and unwittingly plays barometer to our morality.

The sex symbols, those Hollywood stars who come to mean more to us than the characters they play, can sum up an entire generation's sexual attitude. More often than not, the image we associate with these people is just that—an image cooked up by studio heads or publicity hounds determined to plug into the consciousness of the culture—and get rich off of it.

The first openly sexual woman on screen had to be bad, really *evil*; that was the only way audi-

ences at the time would ever have accepted her. William Fox, one of the earliest movie moguls, was well aware of this as he set out to create the first movie sex goddess. He transformed Theodosia Goodman, a tailor's unremarkable daughter from Ohio, into Theda Bara, the cinema's first "vamp" (short for vampire). Theda Bara gripped the public's fevered imagination as a mysterious, man-eating she-devil in roles like Salome, Camille, and Cleopatra—her face a ghastly white, her eyes ringed with deep black, her body barely concealed behind gilded cones and see-through veils.

Fox's publicity machine worked overtime, cranking out a ridiculous background for Bara. She was a princess, the offspring of an Arab sheik; her name was an anagram of ARAB DEATH. To

protect his investment in her image, Fox signed Bara to a contract stipulating, among other things, that she not marry within three years; that she remain "heavily veiled in public"; that she not take public transportation; and, finally, that she only go out at night. Titillated Victorian audiences flocked to see the very first femme fatale do her evil. They had plenty to see; she made forty films in four years.

By 1919, the vamp image in cinema fell from vogue. With her sexual allure no longer of use to him, Fox dropped Bara; after helping establish Fox as a major studio, poor Theda Bara was put out to pasture.

When the twenties came roaring in, audiences were ready for a sexy woman who wasn't evil, and Clara Bow was "It."

As a young girl, Clara Bow went to movies to escape from her harsh childhood in Brooklyn, New York, where she lived with her schizophrenic-epileptic mother and drunkard father. She held on tight to her belief that the "Fame and Fortune" contest in *Motion Picture* magazine offered her an escape route from her bleak life. In 1921, she actually won the contest as well as an opportunity to appear in a real feature film.

Her mother, convinced of the depraved nature of movie people, was obsessed with stopping Bow from pursuing a life of sin and tried to cut her daughter's throat while she slept. Bow awoke just in time, and her screams of terror supposedly snapped her mother out of her murderous trance.

Theda Bara, the original vamp, in Cleopatra, *1917 (opposite), and* Carmen, *1915 (above).*

Above: Clara Bow ("Young America Rampant") with Gilbert Roland and Donald Keith in The Plastic Age, *1925. Opposite: The first dark-skinned leading man in movies, Rudolph Valentino, sporting his famed bolero jacket from* The Four Horsemen of the Apocalypse.

But fame took its toll. Bow's *Wings* costar, Buddy Rogers, noted, "She had always put on this act because she was so shy and insecure. Now Clara believed she was 'the It Girl.' She tried to be vivacious, she tried to be fascinating, she tried to be clever, and she just worked her body and mind and soul to death."

She attracted scandal, too: In her attempts to be "It," she took many lovers, and rumors spread of late-night romps with the entire University of Southern California Trojans football team; in *Photoplay* magazine she recounted her life story, and Hollywood was shocked to have the giggling, bubbly "It" Girl linked with insanity and poverty. An affair with a married man had to be hushed up with studio money, but not before the press found out about the relationship and the arrangement and told all.

The final straw came in 1928, when a scandal rag, *The Coast Reporter*, published graphic accounts of Bow's alleged exhibitionism, kinkiness, incest, lesbianism, and even bestiality, reporting that she had sex with her pet Great Dane, Duke.

The publisher of the rag was thrown in jail for eight years under pornography laws, but not before Bow suffered a nervous breakdown. She attempted a comeback in 1932 with the lurid *Call Her Savage*, but her time was up. The "It" Girl was no longer "It."

The silent cinema also boasted the world's first male sex god, remembered as vividly today as he was idolized then: Rudolph Valentino. Although Valentino was a man, he was seldom free from the scandal and exploitation that surrounded most female sex symbols.

Contrary to the various tales Valentino told to build a romantic past for himself, he was actually a simple Italian peasant who immigrated to the United States in 1913. Once he arrived, the dark, handsome young man found easy work as a high society gigolo, dancing with wealthy ladies at posh New York nightclubs like Maxim's. It was there he learned to move and speak with the grace that would later arouse sexual longing in millions of women.

Bow did escape eventually, when producer B. P. Schulberg brought her out to Hollywood. He proceeded to "loan out" his new starlet for $500 a week (of which she kept $200). She quickly rose to stardom. By 1925, *Motion Picture Classic*, a magazine Clara Bow poured over as a child in Brooklyn, put her on its cover declaring "the truth is little Clara Bow shows alarming symptoms of becoming the sensation of the year in Hollywood. She is the spirit of youth. She is Young America rampant, the symbol of flapperdom."

The Plastic Age, a film released that same year, earned her a contract with Paramount Pictures, which had recently purchased the rights to Elinor Glyn's flapper novel, *It*. Paramount paid the author $50,000 to endorse their new star, Clara Bow, as the one who had "It." Glyn gladly did so, and the film made Bow the ranking Jazz Baby of the Jazz Age, depicting her as a girl-next-door type with a flagrant female sexuality—previously a foreign and decadent attribute.

Richard [Gere] has become a big star based on his attraction for women. He's got a pinup image—which he hates, and I understand that. The only trouble is, whenever they ask him to take his trousers off, he does.

—Michael Caine

But even at this early point in his life scandal found Valentino. He became involved with a married woman, Bianca De Saulles, whom he helped secure a divorce from her husband, Jack. Later, when the woman shot and killed De Saulles, her lawyer recommended Valentino quickly and quietly get out of town. He headed for Hollywood.

Valentino was soon working in pictures, typecast as a heavy because of his dark hair and complexion. And again, it wasn't long before he was involved with a young woman, a blond actress named Jean Acker. They were married within weeks, but Valentino's bliss was short-lived. The night of the wedding, Acker locked him out of their suite, telling him the wedding was off. She had changed her mind, saying she had only married Valentino because she "pitied him."

Valentino, reeling from the blow, nevertheless managed to land a leading role in *The Four Horsemen of the Apocalypse*, a smash hit which turned him into the first dark-skinned leading man in movies and pushed the bolero and the tango into vogue around the world.

The movie also captured the attention of Natacha Rombova, a mysterious Hollywood social climber and an occasional set designer who took on the daily management of Valentino's business affairs as well as

his social life. She tried in vain to talk him out of appearing in a new film called *The Sheik*. Against her wishes he played the title role—the most successful of his career—and created a virtual tidal wave of worship among female moviegoers. Males, too, found a role model in Valentino, the screen's greatest lover; suddenly, women across the country had to fight off new "sheiks"—men who now slicked back their hair and tried to woo them with heavy-lidded, lusty looks. (If only these guys had known how easy that heavy-lidded look was for Valentino; a deadened nerve caused his left eye to droop.)

Valentino persuaded Natacha to marry him, before properly annulling his marriage to Jean Acker; this brought charges of bigamy. He had to swear in court that the new marriage was not consummated, and the newlyweds had to live apart for one year. A few short years later, after he had showered her with antiques, horses, a fleet of cars, and successively larger mansions, Natacha sued Valentino for divorce, claiming the "world's greatest lover" was "too domesticated."

And things just kept getting worse; a Chicago journalist linked Valentino with a growing trend toward effeminacy in American males, supposedly indicated by the sudden popularity of "Pink Powder Puff" cologne dispensers in men's washrooms all over the country.

The end came early for Valentino, who died of peritonitis following a burst appendix in 1926. He was only thirty-one. His death set off mass female hysteria that led a one-time leading lady of his, Alice Terry, to later say "the biggest thing Valentino ever did was to die."

If Theda Bara and Clara Bow were studio-created phenomena, Mae West took every bit of responsibility for her sex goddess image. West, another Brooklyn gal, came up quickly through the ranks of vaudeville. After starting to work in show business at sixteen, West worked at a persona, pulling elements from successful acts of the day—the large ego of a bawdy woman performer, the biting double entendre of a female impersonator. By 1913 she was a suc-

> [Silent] movies were rarely written. In 1927 they were yelled into existence in conferences that kept going in saloons, brothels, and all-night poker games.
>
> — Ben Hecht, screenwriter

cessful solo act, although somewhat misunderstood: She was hailed by critics of the day as America's leading female impersonator.

West left vaudeville behind for a successful career on Broadway and in 1926 wrote her own hit show that she dared to title *Sex*. She and the producer were fined $500 and thrown in jail for ten days for "corrupting the young," but West kept pushing, and it wasn't long before Hollywood called. West was nearly forty when she became the next Hollywood sex goddess.

West was one of the first stars to demand, and get, story approval and credit as well as complete control over production. When remonstrated for writing scripts wherein she got

the only good lines, she responded, "Let Shakespeare do it his way. I'll do it mine. We'll see who comes out better." All this confidence was not misplaced. West wielded her power well, and enjoyed a long and fruitful career. She brought a long string of popular films to the screen, including *She Done Him Wrong*, *I'm No Angel*, *Klondike Annie*, and *My Little Chickadee* (in which she was paired with the great W.C. Fields).

She lived a flamboyant lifestyle in her white-on-white, satin-lined Hollywood apartment and entertained a long list of lovers beneath the mirror she had suspended above her satin-sheeted bed—mostly body builders, wrestlers, and boxers, both black and white.

In 1943 she returned to the stage, reviving and playing in her Broadway sensation *Diamond Lil* throughout the forties and fifties.

Incredibly, she returned to the screen triumphantly twenty-seven years later opposite Raquel Welch in *Myra Breckinridge*, still a master

of the rapid-fire double entendre and still very much a guardian of the image that made her rich and famous.

While Mae West talked about sex and made it fun, her contemporary, the young, curvy blond, Jean Harlow, was sex to every red-blooded male during the thirties.

Harlow had eloped to Hollywood with a wealthy Chicago boy at the age of sixteen. The marriage didn't last, but she wanted to stay, and her parents moved out to join her. She got some extra work and appeared in several Hal Roach comedies, but she wasn't really noticed until Howard Hughes signed her up for his World War I flying aces epic, *Hell's Angels*. In it she plays a woman who wears low-cut gowns, takes on both heroes, and grabs a third guy as well. Despite the picture's extreme dullness, it was the top money-maker of the year, thanks to Harlow's blatant, sizzling sexuality. She became an instant star.

Before Harlow, dark-haired women were considered sexy, while blondes were considered virginal, washed-out, and plain. Harlow changed all that, starting a platinum blonde craze—soon after the film's release, over one hundred cities in America boasted Platinum Blonde Clubs.

Playing gangster molls or tramps (she was the first woman to be called a "tramp" on film, in 1931's *Goldie*), Harlow perfected the wise-cracking, predatory blonde. She was paired with the biggest stars of the day, including Spencer Tracy, Cary Grant, and Clark Gable. She made her impact wearing slinky white satin evening gowns with no underwear and reportedly rubbed ice on her nipples to make them stand out before scenes were shot. She also dyed her pubic hair to match her glittering platinum coif.

But the woman every male lusted after was a sexual paradox. Off the set she lived a childlike existence, preferring carnivals and games of musical chairs to parties or Hollywood nightlife; in reality, Harlow showed little interest in sex, choosing to spend the majority of her spare time with her mother.

Harlow was yet another sex symbol who was haunted by scandal and had been used by the

Left: Jean Harlow, the wise-cracking, predatory platinum blonde in Goldie. Opposite: Every GI's all-American dream gal in the forties, Betty Grable, featured here in a studio publicity still promulgating her "million-dollar legs."

men in her life. Her stepfather, hoping to secure a position with the mob, arranged dates for her with mobster Bugsy Siegel and his friends; her second husband, studio executive Paul Bern, married "the most beautiful woman in the world" in a pitiful attempt to compensate for his impotency.

To the relief of critics and fans, she proved herself a competent comedic actress, allaying fears that she would languish in stereotypical tramp roles and fade away. Unfortunately, her career was cut short; she died of uremic poisoning in 1937, at the age of twenty-six.

The heiress to the sex-goddess throne Harlow left vacant came into her own during World War II, when millions of GIs idolized her as the girl back home they all were fighting for.

Betty Grable was a reluctant star, the victim of an obsessed stage mother who had Betty trained in saxophone, piano, trap drums, ballet, tap dancing, and acrobatics—all by the time she was seven years old. Her mother changed Betty's school records to hide the fact that she never went to school beyond the seventh grade; then she left her husband and second daughter in St. Louis and took young Betty to Hollywood with the intent of making her a star.

By 1933, Betty's mother got her a job as a chorus girl at Twentieth Century-Fox, where Betty spent her days learning dance routines; at night her mother often locked her in a closet in their hotel room, then drank and played poker, networking with other stage mothers.

Over the next two years, Betty made pictures for every major studio in town; no one knew quite what to do with her, and stardom remained elusive. Meanwhile, the studios kept printing pinups of her, a common publicity tactic for all starlets at the time.

As World War II began, Betty began a two-year affair with ex-gangster turned gangster-actor George Raft, despite the studio's warnings about her reputation and Raft's connections to mobster Bugsy Siegel. She became a regular at the Hollywood Canteen, where she met bandleader Harry James and began a relationship with him. Raft, jealous of their dating, eventually came to

blows with James at a nightclub. The news traveled fast: cute little Betty Grable, fought over by a dashing matinee idol and the leader of America's hottest band, turned into Hollywood's leading sex symbol over night.

During the war, her famous over-the-shoulder pin-up photo presented a new, modern type of woman. The curvacious, bosomy woman of the thirties was out, and the "no-nonsense, what-you-see-is-what-you-get" brand of sexuality, representing the newly emancipated American woman, was in. Betty was the all-American dream girl; her red lips, blond hair, and big blue eyes adorned nearly everything in the military, from footlockers to bombers to the first atomic test bomb detonated in the United States. Her appeal didn't stop with Americans; folded copies of her pinup were found in the packs of captured German and Japanese soldiers.

By the mid-fifties, the child who was forced into being a star finally decided she'd had enough and retired from Hollywood. She did perform in *Hello, Dolly!* in both Las Vegas and New York, but she never returned to pictures.

A trademark of these early female Hollywood sex symbols was a consistent, outgoing effusiveness. The male standard was set by Gary Cooper, who became the model of the strong, silent type.

Cooper grew up on his family's ranch in Montana, where he learned to rope and ride. When he wandered into Hollywood in the early 1920s seeking extra work, he didn't have to learn anything. He was in great de-

Above: A classic example of the strong, silent type, Gary Cooper, in a 1937 studio portrait. Opposite: "She can't act, she can't talk, but she's terrific," was Louis B. Mayer's first impression of Ava Gardner.

From westerns, Cooper branched out to become one of Hollywood's most enduring romantic leads, and his astute business sense kept him from being tied to any one studio by exclusive contract—a true rarity in the business at the time. He created memorable roles in such great films as *Mr. Deeds Goes to Town*, *Beau Geste*, *Sergeant York*, and *The Pride of the Yankees*, one of the finest baseball films ever made. His career peaked with the incredible *High Noon*, for which he won an Oscar for Best Actor in 1952. He died in 1961, at the age of sixty.

After World War II, another young woman became Hollywood's leading sex goddess.

Ava Gardner practically fell into stardom. While visiting her sister in New York City, Gardner modeled for her brother-in-law, a photographer with a small studio there. Gardner thought nothing of the session and soon returned to her home in North Carolina.

Meanwhile, an MGM New York talent scout passing by the photographer's shop window noticed the photograph and requested some copies. Eventually, a screen test was arranged for Gardner, who, after some coaxing, finally agreed. MGM's New York office filmed her in a silent screen test, knowing their counterparts in Hollywood would never get past her heavy Southern accent.

Hollywood liked what they saw and brought her out to the West Coast for a full-blown screen test at the studio. An hour after stepping off the train in Pasadena, Gardner was dressed in a gown, her hair and makeup done, and she was reading lines before one of the best cinematographers in the business. Mere hours after that, Louis B. Mayer himself reviewed the film, looking for his latest starlet. "She can't act, she can't talk, but she's terrific," he said. Gardner was instantly offered a contract.

Immediately, the studio mechanism sprang into action. She was sent to daily speech lessons to iron out her thick dialect. The studio liked the name Ava Gardner, but told the press her original name was Lucy Ann Johnson, so it would seem that "Ava Gardner" was a studio invention.

mand and, thanks to the early practice of reusing stunt footage in a number of films, Cooper may have appeared in as many as fifty silent westerns before becoming known by name to audiences in *The Winning of Barbara Worth* in 1926.

Cooper's low-key, understated style was perfect for film, and he fared even better with the coming of sound, despite the fact that his first full talkie, *The Virginian*, in 1929, offered him little more dialogue than a simple "yep" or "nope." The film made such an impression that his strong, silent-type image stuck and held fast. This image, coupled with his well-known affairs with Clara Bow and the fiery Lupe Velez brought hordes of women flocking to see his films.

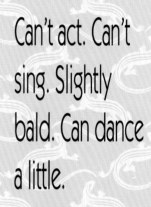

Can't act. Can't sing. Slightly bald. Can dance a little.

— Unknown studio talent executive, on Fred Astaire's screen test

*Above: The fresh-
scrubbed beauty of
Norma Jeane Mortensen,
later Marilyn Monroe,
seen in an early still.*

marriage very soon fell apart. Once the divorce was final, Gardner felt MGM was letting her career slide, passing her over for roles and not actively seeking to loan her out. Reluctantly, MGM loaned her to Universal in 1946 for a film called *The Killers* that was based on a Hemingway story. Her role as the femme fatale Kitty opposite Burt Lancaster made her a star.

After playing Lady Brett Ashley in Hemingway's *The Sun Also Rises*, some say she became the character—a loner who found solace in alcohol. But Gardner continued to make movies into the seventies, never succumbing to self-destruction. She once said, upon retiring to London, that having never overdosed, committed suicide, or died in a car wreck was, in itself, some kind of success to her. Of course, Marilyn Monroe, her successor and the ultimate example of the cinema sex symbol, wasn't quite as successful in that respect.

Marilyn Monroe, formerly Norma Jeane Mortensen, came from the classic sex symbol background, one of parental deprivations and extreme poverty. She never knew her father; her mother and natural grandparents were all committed to mental institutions at one time or another; and her uncle committed suicide. There is one difference between Monroe's upbringing and that of the myriad other sex symbols: Marilyn was a child of Hollywood, born and raised in the world's movie capital.

Monroe was discovered by a publicity photographer on assignment to the aircraft factory where she worked. He noticed her photogenic quality and offered to take some shots. She soon signed with modeling agent Emmeline Snively who, by 1946, had turned Monroe, still known as Norma Jeane Mortensen, into a successful pinup model; she appeared on five magazine covers a month that year alone.

A little white lie sent Monroe on her trip to stardom. She was stricken with a case of appendicitis; during her brief hospital stay, Snively hinted to the press that Howard Hughes (by then, renowned for "discovering" budding sex symbols) had inquired about the model's health.

Within a month of her arrival at MGM, she started dating the hottest young star on the lot, Mickey Rooney. Not long after, they were engaged. Mayer was opposed to the marriage of his biggest star to a starlet who wouldn't even be ready to go before cameras for at least a year. He called Rooney into his office to chew him out. Rooney arrived to plead his case with Gardner at his side. Mayer ignored Gardner and lit into his star—shouting, crying, even pleading that there was a war on—all to no avail. Rooney stood tough and eventually Mayer gave in.

Gardner and Rooney were married six months after Gardner's arrival in Hollywood. Of course, the two had little in common and the

The publicity stunt was enough to get her a much-desired screen test at Twentieth Century-Fox.

The most she got from the ensuing contract was the name Marilyn (Monroe was her grandmother's maiden name) and contacts with several powerful men, such as Harry Cohn and John Huston, who gave her a small role in his hit film, *The Asphalt Jungle*.

Her breakthrough film was *Niagara* in 1953. It was by no means a great movie, but audiences left their televisions to come out and see her. In retrospect, many attribute the film's success to a seventy-foot (21-m) tracking shot of Monroe walking away from the camera in a skintight dress.

In 1954, she married Joe DiMaggio, and it seemed she had reached the apex of the American Dream: voluptuous movie star marries king of the great American pastime.

But the marriage was short-lived. DiMaggio was a jealous, old-fashioned boy, and Monroe's wild lifestyle and the adoration of her fans tore him up. The final straw came in New York on the set of *The Seven Year Itch* when, as DiMaggio watched from down the block, hundreds of New Yorkers cheered as Monroe stood on a subway grate and a wind machine blew her skirt up around her waist.

At this time, Monroe was battling with Twentieth Century-Fox over the sexpot roles she was being given, as she was concerned over the quality of scripts and her general reputation. She refused to cooperate with the studio, which finally suspended her.

Divorced and suspended, she headed back to New York to focus on her acting and to find herself. She studied with Lee and Paula Strasberg at The Actors Studio, hoping to expand her skills and become more than a pinup wiggling her way

through her films. The Strasbergs saw her potential, as well as her frailty, and became surrogate parents to her.

Buoyed by her work in New York, Monroe returned to Hollywood a year later to film *Bus Stop*. Those close to her feared that she might have lost the momentum she had created before she left, but *Bus Stop* was a great success. She then took the opportunity to form her own company, Marilyn Monroe Productions.

In June 1956 she married playwright Arthur Miller, who essentially became her guardian for the next several years; he escorted her to sets and encouraged and supported her. With his help, she completed two films—*The Prince and the Showgirl* and *Some Like It Hot*—before the stress between them grew too great. Her next film was *Let's Make Love*. During the filming, Monroe and costar Yves Montand had a brief affair. But it was enough to prove to both Miller and Monroe that their marriage was over. Before they could split completely, there was one final project Miller had to see her through.

During his time with Monroe, Miller had begun a screenplay based on her, which he

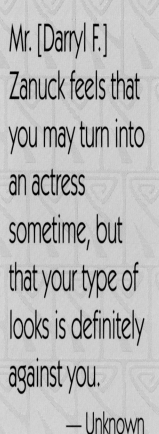

Above:
Marilyn Monroe, the sex symbol who had it all, shown here with then-husband American icon Joe DiMaggio (left) and suave Cary Grant (right).

Above: Clark Gable and Marilyn Monroe in Arthur Miller's The Misfits, *each star's last completed film.*

called *The Misfits*. The couple was divorced as *The Misfits* went into production, but Miller remained on hand during the filming. At one point in the movie, Monroe's costar, Clark Gable, looks down at her and prophetically says, "You're the saddest girl I ever saw." The picture was Gable's last film—and Monroe's as well.

Two years later Monroe was fired from a Twentieth Century-Fox effort called *Something's Got to Give* for failing to show up on time, if at all. Shortly thereafter, depressed, her health and self-confidence waning, she died of an apparent drug overdose in her Brentwood bedroom. (For more on the controversy surrounding her death, see page 151.)

If Monroe was the ideal female of the 1950s, Rock Hudson was her male counterpart. Tall, handsome, well-groomed, well-behaved, he was the perfect, pleasant antidote to his contemporaries—men like Brando and Dean, who

portrayed the vulnerable aspects of men. Rock Hudson, solid when compared to these sufferers, was aptly named.

Hudson became a star in 1954, opposite Jane Wyman in the mythical melodrama *Magnificent Obsession*, as the wayward playboy who turns his life around to atone for his sins. His screen persona thus shifted, Hudson settled in to "good guy" roles, which he played throughout the late fifties and early sixties in a string of fluffy bedroom farces with Doris Day. From *Pillow Talk*, their 1959 film, through *Love, Come Back* in 1961, they waged their oddly bitter, unsettling battle of the sexes, à la Tracy and Hepburn, but without the passion or compassion underneath. Women were titillated by Hudson's cool, polite exterior that hinted at the wolf beneath. Hudson's popularity was a classic reflection of the battle of the times—between conformity on one side and repression on the other.

In Hollywood a girl's virtue is a lot less important than her hairdo.

— Marilyn Monroe

Hudson remained a star on film and television until his death from AIDS in October 1985. The subsequent revelation that he had been homosexual added irony to his career as a longtime symbol of male heterosexuality.

While Marilyn Monroe had put Fox through numerous problems, she did help make the studio a lot of money. Across town at Columbia, notorious studio boss Harry Cohn was smarting after losing his prime sex goddess, Rita Hayworth, through her marriage to Prince Aly Kahn. Cohn needed a blonde to compete with Monroe and put the word out to casting chief Max Arnow to begin the search; the woman he eventually found also happened to be beautiful, curvacious, and named Marilyn.

Recently arrived in Hollywood from the suburbs of Chicago, Marilyn Novak was interested in being a model after a successful stint as Miss Deepfreeze of 1953, demonstrating refrigerators at appliance fairs. She had no desire at all to act in pictures, but her Hollywood modeling agency

thought she was too large for the usual swimsuit and evening gown jobs. Overriding her wishes, they sent her on casting calls for chorus girls.

Arnow spotted Novak in a chorus line and, taken with her beautiful face, got her a screen test. He ran the film for Cohn, who was unimpressed with her talent. "The girl has probably never even read the funnies out loud," he said. "Don't listen, Harry. Just look," replied Arnow.

Cohn gave Novak a short-term contract; for obvious reasons, Marilyn was out of the running as a first name. So Kim Novak was born, almost against her will; she reportedly told friends during those first few weeks at Columbia that she didn't want to be a star—ever.

Cohn was a classic example of the megalomaniac studio boss. His office door had no handles and could only be opened with the push of a button at his desk—no one entered or left unless he said so. He installed a bank of bright lights that shone on those who entered so he could size them up before they did the same to him. He was

Right: Rock Hudson with Jane Wyman in **Magnificent Obsession.** *Women were drawn to Hudson's cool exterior, which suggested that a wolf lay underneath.*

The Cast

Every man I knew
had fallen in love
with "Gilda"
and wakened
with me.

— Rita Hayworth,
on her role
in the
1946 film
of the
same
name

Strip away the phony tinsel of Hollywood and you'll find the real tinsel underneath.

— Oscar Levant

role was the grand dame of sex symbols, Mae West, who by 1970, was in her late seventies. Welch had built a reputation for being difficult on the set, so it was surprising to few that the egos of the two women clashed constantly.

Critics said the film was "tasteless," and the only performance to garner positive comments was West's. At the opening at Radio City Music Hall in New York City, West's limousine was mobbed by cheering, screaming fans; Welch was all but ignored.

Welch, whom a technician once referred to as "silicon from the waist up," has always managed to keep herself in the public eye. Even today, she continues to promote herself, scantily clad in a collection of workout videos.

Raquel Welch was a stepping-stone between the carefully crafted love goddesses of the studios and today's independent actresses who control their own images. Most of these women pursue roles of strength and intelligence, and have effectively lifted themselves out of "bimbo limbo." In fact, most of today's Hollywood actresses, even if they are considered sexy, don't allow themselves to be defined by their physical appearance and work hard to keep from being limited to one kind of persona. These women are tough and demand to be taken seriously, creating female characters on film with more dimension—and sex appeal—than ever before.

The new sex symbols are women like Kathleen Turner, who, with her steely good looks and husky voice, has been called "the thinking man's goddess." Her voice is the product of a childhood spent abroad and attending school in Cuba and Venezuela. Her career took off like a rocket—after eighteen months as a nurse on the soap opera *The Doctors*, Turner auditioned for Lawrence Kasdan's *Body Heat*; she caught the director's eye at the audition by knocking over some ashtrays. She got the part and was a tremendous success as the cool, erotic murderess. She literally walked into stardom.

Turner was instantly besieged by offers to do more sexy bad-girl roles, and while in England to promote the film, she was bashfully asked by

British journalists if she might put on a swimsuit for some photographs. Turner held out and since then has had the opportunity to display an incredibly diverse talent, becoming one of the most versatile actresses in Hollywood. She's played everything from a Mafia hit woman in *Prizzi's Honor* to a spinsterish romance novelist in *Romancing the Stone*.

Today's screen goddesses rarely suffered parental deprivations and impoverished childhoods. Ellen Barkin, for example, sums up her early years in two simple phrases: "Happy childhood. No divorces." And unlike the virtual studio slaves of Hollywood past, Barkin lives with her husband Gabriel Byrne and their young son in New York or their home in Ireland, coming to Hollywood only when it becomes necessary.

Barkin studied acting from age fifteen to twenty-six before she was finally coaxed into auditioning. She has been working ever since. Her steamy sex scenes in three hit movies—with Dennis Quaid in *The Big Easy*, Al Pacino in *Sea of*

Above: Kathleen Turner, "the thinking man's goddess," sweats it out with Michael Douglas in 1984's **Romancing the Stone.**

Opposite: Ellen Barkin, star of the steamy thriller Sea of Love. *Above: The "Sexiest Man Alive" according to* People *magazine in 1985, Mel Gibson.*

Gibson was born in Peekskill, New York, in 1951, and moved to Australia with his family at the age of twelve. After graduating from school, he had vague aspirations to journalism but didn't pursue them. In fact, he pursued very little. It was his sister who sent his photograph and application fee to the Australian National Institute of Dramatic Art. The Institute granted the surprised young man an audition and later accepted him.

Gibson excelled as an acting student. Shortly after graduation, he was cast in *Mad Max*, a postapocalyptic biker flick that became the most popular movie ever to come out of Australia. A few years later, its sequel, *The Road Warrior*, blasted Gibson into worldwide stardom. He proceeded to make six movies in the next three years—four of them in 1984 alone—including the *Road Warrior* sequel, *Beyond Thunder Dome*. This streak of appearances brought his fame to a crescendo, prompting the aforementioned *People* magazine comment, as well as Gibson's rebuttal in *Vanity Fair* when asked if the declaration troubled him. "Nah," he told the magazine, "It's one of those things that could become an obstacle if you let it. I ignore it."

During this busy time, Gibson began drinking more heavily than usual. The work and the drink took its toll on him. He retired to his eight hundred-acre (324-ha) cattle ranch in Australia in 1982, rested, and returned triumphantly to the screen in the megahit *Lethal Weapon*, opposite Danny Glover, in 1984. His bankability has continued to climb ever since, and the star of such hits as *Tequila Sunrise* and *Lethal Weapon II* now commands upwards of $4 million per picture.

Perhaps Clara Bow, at the height of the roaring twenties, was really nothing like "It," and it's possible another man living in 1985 had more sex appeal than Mel Gibson. Perhaps these sex symbols were not the best actors ever to grace the screen, or even the most well-adjusted group in film history, but they did, and still do, mean something to us. They reflect, in their shimmering film images and, at times, in the real lives they lead, our highest physical and emotional ideals for men and women in our time.

Love, and Mickey Rourke in *Johnny Handsome*—have turned this talented actress with offbeat good looks into a sex symbol of the times.

Few men have reached such acclaimed sex-symbol status as Mel Gibson, an actor *People* magazine proclaimed "The Sexiest Man Alive" in 1985. Few would argue that he has relinquished the title to someone else in the years since.

It's better than being a pimp.
— Harry Cohn, on being a studio boss

Love Lives

part two

CHAPTER FOUR

Dating Games

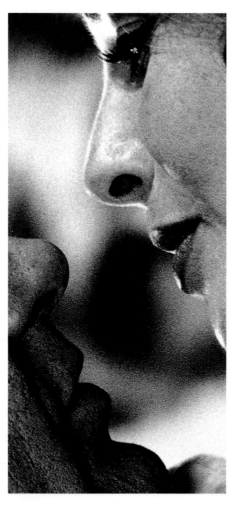

Fame sure is fickle. A Hollywood star might be sitting on top of the world one day and be well on the way to obscurity the next. There can be any number of causes for a plummet from fame—a string of bad movies (or even *one* real stinker), unpopular politics, or a simple change in vogue. So fame has to be nurtured, helped along. Long ago, studio publicity people discovered the secret to keeping faltering stars in the public eye: romance. They took to promoting Hollywood romances for everything they were worth.

Stars in Hollywood's heyday of the thirties and forties were routinely "linked romantically" with so many others that it would be nearly impossible (let alone meaningless) to try to untangle the supposed crisscrossing lines of attraction. As an example, take unlikely ladies' man James Stewart, who was "linked romantically" with some 263 glamour girls before leaving for the U.S. Air Force in World War II. The public relations departments of the major studios were working overtime to stage-manage these phony romances, illustrating the incredible publicity drawing power of two stars in love.

The studios spent nearly as much time covering up the actual sex lives of the stars—and offering them alternatives. Between 1935 and 1940, several major studios operated their own cathouses and asked their male stars to visit these to avoid the unnecessary risk of sexually transmitted diseases. The women, all beautiful, young, rejected starlets, were examined regularly by studio doctors.

This is not to say that true romance between stars is rare. In fact, romance is a common vocational hazard in the movie business. Hollywood *is* glamour and romance, and the stars who bring all that to the screen make their living through seduction while being reminded daily of their sex appeal. The fact that they work closely with one another for long periods of time, often with very emotional material, makes on-set romances almost a certainty.

Actual romances occur almost as frequently as the fictitious ones created by the public relations machines. There was the sizzling true romance between Greta Garbo and John Gilbert on the set of *Flesh and the Devil;* Clark Gable was renowned for cavorting off-camera with his on-camera partners, such as Joan Crawford in *Dance, Fools, Dance,* Elizabeth Allen in *Men in White,* and Loretta Young in *The Call of the Wild;* and Bette Davis made time with George Brent while filming *Dark Victory.*

But love doesn't always come easy, even in the dream capital. William Holden carried a torch for the young Audrey Hepburn for decades, but she never considered him more than a good friend. The rebuffed Holden later recounted setting "off around the world with the idea of screwing a woman in every country I visited, and I succeeded." Hepburn was not impressed.

The tradition of hanky-panky between stars reaches as far back as the silent days of film. John Barrymore seduced young Mary Astor during their "rehearsals" in his apartment while the teenager's mother was sent to sip tea out on the veranda. And some Hollywood stars seemed to consider sleeping around a second career (or perhaps an integral part of their first). These people developed reputations around Hollywood that have become legendary.

Gary Cooper, one of the top leading men during the thirties and forties, had plenty of success off-camera, too. Clara Bow, who some hold responsible for advancing Cooper's career, used to call him "Studs." She once told Hedda Hopper that Cooper was "hung like a horse and can go all night!" Many more female stars would try and cor-

roborate her story over his decades in Hollywood, including Patricia Neal, his costar in *The Fountainhead;* Lupe Velez; Carole Lombard; and Marlene Dietrich (who was also infamous for a long line of affairs, even though she had married and never divorced).

Cooper wasn't alone. Other stars such as John Wayne, John Gilbert, and Eddie Fisher were equally prolific in their romantic pursuits. But perhaps the greatest Hollywood playboy in the Golden Age was Errol Flynn, whose swashbuckling and amorous adventures on the screen pale in comparison to the life he really lived.

According to biographer Charles Higham in *Errol Flynn: The Untold Story,* Flynn was determined to live life to its fullest and experience every pleasure to the limit, and he managed to do so for decades under the extremely scrutinizing and critical eye of the Hollywood community. He led a virtually secret life that

Opposite: The classic big-screen romance—Liz Taylor and Richard Burton in Who's Afraid of Virginia Woolf? *Above: Marlene Dietrich was infamous for a long line of affairs despite the fact that she had married and never divorced.*

included prostitutes, homosexual trysts, under-aged boys and girls, voyeurism, and Nazi spy rings in his quest for "experience" and excitement.

Despite this wild life (or perhaps as a cover for it), Flynn married three times. His first marriage was to sophisticated French actress Lili Damita, whom he would taunt by emptying his pockets onto his nightstand, creating a neat little pile of his wallet, keys, change . . . and condoms. He was married a second time to a young woman named Nora Eddington, who caught Flynn's eye as she was selling cigarettes and gum in the lobby of the Hall of Justice during his trial for statutory rape. They were wed by proxy in Mexico eight months after Nora became pregnant. Later, at age forty-one, Flynn married the twenty-four-year-old Patrice Wymore. Eventually they separated, and at the age of fifty, Flynn was finally paired with a young woman many believe was his only true love—the fifteen-year-old Beverly Aadland. If Flynn had lived to see her turn a legal age, perhaps they, too, would have tied the knot.

But it was outside his marriages that Flynn sought his thrills. More often than not, he found them aboard his yacht, *Sirocco*, to which women would flock in the hope of making love with the great screen idol. To crew or friends who helped him satisfy the vast numbers of sex-hungry women, Flynn would present a silver lapel pin in the shape of a penis and testicles with the insignia 'F.F.F.' (short for "Flynn's Flying Fuckers"). Contests were held nightly and score was kept. Flynn always came away the victor.

Flynn's yachts also carried him away to adventure. Fed up with the constant bickering with studios and directors, Flynn would stock the *Sirocco* for a scientific or geographic excursion and set sail, spending months at sea, coming ashore in distant ports to restock his liquor supply and sample the local women. On one such voyage to Venezuela and Argentina, Flynn met Eva Perón and, fascinated with her fascism, began a secret four-year affair with her. Acapulco was another frequent stop on Flynn's travels. It was there he went to satiate his homosexual urges with his private beachboy, Apollonio Diaz. In fact, it was in Mexico, removed from the prudish movie colony, that Flynn engaged in nearly all of his

Right: Errol Flynn and former cigarette girl Nora Eddington. She became Flynn's second wife by proxy after she became pregnant with his child. Opposite: Flynn, his third bride, Patrice Wymore, and their six-month-old daughter, Annela.

MORE ON-SCREEN/ OFFSCREEN ROMANCES

Ellen Barkin and Gabriel Byrne in *Siesta*

Kim Basinger and Alec Baldwin in *The Marrying Man*

Kim Basinger and Prince in *Batman*

Matthew Broderick and Jennifer Grey in *Ferris Bueller's Day Off*

Matthew Broderick and Helen Hunt in *WarGames*

Tom Cruise and Rebecca DeMornay in *Risky Business*

Tom Cruise and Nicole Kidman in *Days of Thunder*

Marion Davies and Dick Powell in *Hearts Divided*

Geena Davis and Jeff Goldblum in *The Fly*

Laura Dern and Kyle MacLachlan in *Blue Velvet*

Marlene Dietrich and Gary Cooper in *Morocco*

Marlene Dietrich and James Stewart in *Destry Rides Again*

William Hurt and Marlee Matlin in *Children of a Lesser God*

homosexual activity. There too Flynn's tryst with matinee idol Tyrone Power took place. The affair didn't last, but the two stars apparently became fast friends.

Of course, not all of Flynn's amorous adventures happened aboard ship or abroad. In fact, he designed his famous hilltop mansion, Mulholland Farm, to accommodate his special tastes. His appetite for watching two men have sex while he made love to a woman was satisfied via the infamous system of two-way mirrors he had installed in the house. His bawdy sense of humor was expressed in the decorating details: his liquor cabinet displayed a bullfighting scene (to open the cabinet one pushed the bull's testicles); the trick chairs from which large, quivering foam rubber penises would spring; and his giant bed surrounded with black silk curtains adorned with golden question marks.

The place was Flynn's dream house and was where many of his wilder dreams came to life. He acquired entire groups of prostitutes for a night, and he and his friends would watch the nocturnal action from above through two-way mirrors that

were suspended over the top of the beds. Nora, his wife at the time, was mercifully set up at a different house.

Flynn didn't see these deviations as wrong. He simply lusted for life. And he wasn't selfish about it; he wanted everyone to live life to the fullest. It must have been that attitude that prompted Flynn to give his son, Sean, a present for his twelfth birthday he'd never forget—his first visit to a whorehouse.

While Flynn, the great Hollywood playboy of the thirties and forties, managed somewhat successfully to keep his philandering out of the public eye, Frank Sinatra, the next reigning Hollywood playboy, was less successful. Sinatra's private philandering often became public knowledge, creating in him a vehement hatred of reporters and the press.

Sinatra's popularity as a crooner began to fade after World War II, as his bobby-soxer fans turned to the new rock and roll. But he found his salvation in the movies and made a truly great comeback. He also achieved a well-earned reputation as a notorious womanizer. He has dated a

The public has always expected me to be a playboy, and a decent chap never lets his public down.

— Errol Flynn

Below: Frank Sinatra finally wins over Ava Gardner. The cutting of their wedding cake may have been one of the few happy moments in their brief, troubled relationship.

long line of starlets, models, vocalists, and chorus girls, among them Anita Ekberg, Kim Novak, and Lisa Ferraday, and has several high-profile marriages under his belt.

The love of his life, in the opinion of those close to Sinatra, was Ava Gardner. The two met while they were both under contract at MGM. Sinatra was separated from his first wife, Nancy, and was steadily making his way through a master list of MGM actresses he had tacked to the back of his dressing room door. Gardner was struggling to get back on her feet after

a disastrous second marriage to bandleader Artie Shaw. The two MGM contract players immediately began a troubled relationship, troubled because Gardner was leery of having anything to do with Sinatra, and she went so far as to call him a hoodlum. Ironically, her cool treatment only pulled Sinatra in deeper; he tended to mistreat women who loved him and fell hard for those who rejected him. Sinatra and Gardner were married on November 7, 1951.

As quickly as it began, the Gardner-Sinatra relationship soured. One night, while they were both working in New York, Sinatra had heard that his wife was out with her ex-husband, Artie Shaw, patching up their friendship. Sinatra tracked them down, calling from the Hampshire House Hotel, and got her on the phone. When she answered, he told her he was going to kill himself and fired a pistol. Panic-stricken, Gardner rushed to the hotel only to find the desperate Sinatra had fired the gun into his mattress. Sinatra's obsession became too much for her, and in the autumn of 1953, Gardner divorced Ole Blue Eyes and took up residence in Spain to avoid his violent temper and possessiveness.

Unrequited love didn't stop Sinatra from playing the field and showering the women he loved and left with gifts to compensate for his guilt, as he did when he began dating Judy Garland in the fifties, not long after her breakup with Vincente Minnelli. Eventually he stood her up, moving on to other women. Three weeks later when Garland was hospitalized for "exhaustion," Sinatra bombarded her with flowers and phone calls every day.

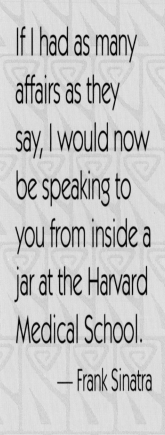

If I had as many affairs as they say, I would now be speaking to you from inside a jar at the Harvard Medical School.

— Frank Sinatra

Sinatra also helped Joe DiMaggio try to get some dirt on Marilyn Monroe to further his divorce case—a fiasco that became known as "The Wrong Door Case" (Sinatra and DiMaggio broke down the door of the wrong apartment while trying to catch Monroe in a "lesbian" act). After Monroe and DiMaggio split for good, Sinatra started dating her. Later, DiMaggio refused to allow Sinatra to attend the tragic star's funeral.

In similar fashion, Sinatra began an affair with Lauren Bacall that flared into a real romance after Humphrey Bogart's death in 1957. Bacall wanted marriage, and in March 1958, Sinatra finally proposed. The next day he flew off to Miami for a show, and Bacall took in a play with agent Swifty Lazar. Leaving the theater, a reporter asked Bacall about the possibility of marriage to Sinatra; a

headline in the early edition of the next day's *Los Angeles Examiner* read: SINATRA TO MARRY BACALL. Bacall telephoned Sinatra in Miami to let him know the word was out, but he already knew— reporters had surrounded his hotel and he was furious. He suggested they lay low for a while until things calmed down. He didn't speak to her again for six years, and then only in anger.

The next big romance for Sinatra began with Mia Farrow's infatuation with him. While Sinatra (then forty-nine years old) filmed *Von Ryan's Express* in 1964, he noticed that the petite nineteen-year-old actress made daily visits to the set to stare in awe at him. Eventually she got up the nerve to speak to him and his entourage as they passed by her. She had overheard that they were heading out to Sinatra's Palm Springs compound

Above: Sinatra had a reason to smile; of Mia Farrow he said: "I finally found a broad I can cheat on."

for the weekend and invited herself along. Sinatra laughed and said she could join them if she wanted to.

Sinatra and Farrow quickly became an item, and Sinatra soon was entertaining notions of marrying the young actress. He casually put the idea to his close friend, Brad Dexter, asking him if he thought it was a good idea. Dexter thought the May-December marriage was a bad idea and said so. Sinatra became irate, throwing furniture and breaking lamps. He picked up a phone and ordered Farrow to Las Vegas on the next plane from London. He joined her there the next day and they were married.

These were not ideal circumstances for beginning a life together, but Sinatra was happy.

Shortly after the marriage, during one of his Vegas shows, he asked his new wife to stand and introduced her, saying, "I finally found a broad I can cheat on."

Causing even more friction in the relationship was Farrow's acting career; Sinatra didn't like the idea that his wife made a living from acting. He reportedly beat her for accepting roles in films and threatened filmmakers who dared to cast her. While she was away from Hollywood making *Rosemary's Baby*, Sinatra called her and ordered her to return to his side. She refused, explaining that she still had a month's work to do on the picture. The next day, Sinatra's attorney arrived on the *Rosemary* set and asked to speak with her. Inside her dressing room he served her with divorce papers.

So far, Sinatra has tied the knot only once more, with a woman who lived near his Palm Springs complex—Barbara Marx, an ex-chorus girl and the former wife of Zeppo Marx. She saw Sinatra's lifestyle as a distinct step up from Marx's modest wealth; she eventually divorced Marx and moved in with Sinatra. Afterward, Sinatra slowed down somewhat. By that time, movie fans were more interested in the legendary amorous adventures of the master of the form, Warren Beatty.

Even before Beatty made his first movie, *Splendor in the Grass*—the 1961 picture that made him a star—he had acquired a reputation as a ladies' man. After moving West and working his way through a crop of nameless starlets, he set his sights on sex goddess Joan Collins, who played the role to the limit—she once appeared in public in a gown so tight that she had to be carried up the stairs to make an appearance. Beatty's pursuit was successful, and he and Collins began a highly visible affair. Collins was once quoted as saying that Beatty was insatiable, that "three, four, five times a day, every day, was not unusual for him. He was also able to accept phone calls at the same time." There were rumors that the two were engaged by the time Beatty went to work on *Splendor* with Natalie Wood.

The timing was right (or wrong, depending on your point of view) because Wood and her

THE GARDEN OF ALLAH

During the Golden Age of Hollywood the Garden of Allah Hotel, twenty-five bungalows and a main building built around a pool at the corner of Crescent Heights and Sunset Boulevard, was the center of Hollywood nightlife, a bastion of intellectual and sexual pleasures—the rowdy, drunken heart of the movie colony. Here is a short list of the greats who lived at "the Garden" between January 1927, when it was opened by Alla Nazimova, and August 1959, when it was finally torn down (the site is now a mini-mall):

Greta Garbo lived there upon her arrival in Hollywood, as did brilliant comedy director Ernst Lubitsch.

John Barrymore lived there between marriages; Gilbert Roland courted Clara Bow in her villa at the Garden.

Laurence Olivier stayed at the Garden while in town to screen-test opposite Garbo in *Queen Christina*—Garbo, by the way, refused to even view his test.

Charles and Elsa Laughton lived there for years and, when they did eventually move to a home of their own, it was only blocks away.

Artie Shaw resided there during his brief marriage to Ava Gardner, and Errol Flynn and Humphrey Bogart were residents between their various marriages. David Niven shared a room with Flynn during his early days in Hollywood.

F. Scott Fitzgerald stayed at the Garden during his last futile attempt to write for the movies.

Other notable guests included: John Carradine, Johnny Carson, Marlene Dietrich, Jackie Gleason, Ruth Gordon, George S. Kaufman, Buster Keaton, Burgess Meredith, Frank Sinatra, and Orson Welles.

husband, Robert Wagner, were going through a rocky time in their new marriage. The handsome Beatty, working side by side with the beautiful Natalie Wood, couldn't resist the temptation, and shortly after the film was completed, they were seen out together. The press took great interest in the whole messy situation and hounded all parties involved, driving Joan Collins to publicly deny she and Beatty were ever engaged to be married. It was this flurry of press attention that drove Beatty, from that time on, to refuse to answer press questions about his personal life.

The affair with Wood did not last, and the next actress of any stature to be associated with Beatty was Leslie Caron. Beatty and Caron were seen in public, despite the fact that Caron was going through a bitter divorce from her second husband, Peter Hall, who had officially cited Beatty in the divorce papers. Eventually Caron and Beatty split up, too. Many believe she was wary of entering into a third marriage.

By the mid-sixties, Beatty had become the consummate Hollywood bachelor, living without family or domestic ties of any kind. He lived for months on end in a small room in the Beverly Wilshire Hotel that was cluttered with scripts, newspapers, and unopened mail; he drove rented cars and entertained a long line of women who came and went with great frequency.

In 1967, he began a relationship with actress Julie Christie, his costar in the 1971 film *McCabe and Mrs. Miller*. Observers thought this was *it*, that Beatty and Christie were sure to be married, but shortly after the film was released, so was Beatty. Apparently, he had become too blatant with his womanizing and Christie had had enough.

After that, Beatty released *Shampoo*, a film he cowrote with Robert Towne. The film's promiscuous lead role of the hairdresser George was seen by critics as an attempt by Beatty to prove that he wasn't a misogynist or latent homosexual.

The romance style of the New Hollywood in the early seventies would have seemed strange to many stars from Hollywood's Golden Age (and that's saying something!). It was more insular and closed off—the relationships took on an almost

incestuous quality. Beatty, for instance, began a relationship with Michelle Phillips, from the pop group the Mamas and the Papas. Phillips had already made the rounds of Beatty's friends, having been through a quickie marriage to Beatty's pal, Hollywood wild man Dennis Hopper, and a two-year romance with Hopper and Beatty's friend, Jack Nicholson, before

Above: Warren Beatty restraining himself with costar Natalie Wood in Splendor in the Grass.

Above: Beatty with his latest costar/lover, Annette Bening. The couple married in January 1992 and have a baby daughter, Kathlyn Bening Beatty.

book movie *Dick Tracy*. But once the film was released and the public relations machine was unplugged, Beatty and Madonna were seen out with other people and talking about what a "good friend" the other was.

After three decades of dominating the gossip columns as Hollywood's preeminent bachelor, Beatty has finally found time to build a permanent residence, a mansion high atop Mulholland Drive furnished with rental furniture and a piano, not far from the home of his friend Jack Nicholson. Few believe Beatty will settle there for long, although he and *Bugsy* costar Annette Bening recently had a baby daughter and were married shortly thereafter.

Although the gossip pages continue to follow the romantic inclinations of stars quite carefully, and they never lack for material, Beatty seems to be the last of the true Hollywood playboys. Some current stars, both male and female, are nipping at his heels, but perhaps Sylvester Stallone comes closest to taking the lead.

Stallone came West after struggling along in New York City, supporting his wife, Sasha, with the occasional acting job, including a stint in a soft-core pornography film. They drove out to Hollywood in a junk car and set up house in a cheap apartment by the freeway. Their money dwindled lower and lower. Meanwhile, Stallone had decided to try and make it as a writer and began peddling a little idea he had about a small-time boxer who becomes the champ. *Rocky* was made and became an amazing success that launched the actor into worldwide fame and fortune. Soon Stallone was straying from home, dating international fashion model Susan Anton. Stallone moved out of his home and Anton left her husband to move in with him. Twice Stallone backed down and returned to Sasha, but he couldn't stay away from Anton. The third time he left and tried to return, he found Sasha had locked and chained the door. Unfortunately for him, Anton, too, had enough of the yo-yoing Stallone and let him go.

Now Stallone was not only rich and famous, he was available.

rebounding into Beatty's arms. Things seemed to be going well with the couple until Phillips began pushing for marriage.

Later, Beatty's affairs began to take on the appearance of career moves; his lengthy affair with actress Diane Keaton seemed, again, to be one that might culminate in marriage. The two triumphed in Beatty's dream project, *Reds*, and went their separate ways shortly thereafter. More recently, rumors of romance swirled around Beatty and Madonna, his costar in the comic-

[Jack Nicholson] and Beatty have contests about it.

— Bruce Dern, on his two friends' womanizing

Right: Sylvester Stallone out and about with model Jennifer Flavin.

Soon after his divorce from Sasha, a statuesque Nordic blonde, Brigitte Nielsen, called Stallone and said her life's goal was to meet the star. He agreed to meet her and, although he was a little put off by her aggressiveness, fell for her attentions. They were married almost right away; but the marriage lasted all of 548 days. Stallone managed to get her a role in *Beverly Hills Cop II* with Eddie Murphy, and it wasn't long before the rumors began flying. Nielsen was "linked romantically" with everyone from Murphy to the director Tony Scott to her female gym instructor. Those close to Stallone never did see what he saw in her. Nielsen walked away with a reported $6 million settlement.

Once his divorce proceedings began, Stallone launched into what gossip papers said could only be called a "dating frenzy." He was seen with a different tall, young, and usually blonde woman every other week for a year. Some were well known, such as game-show hostess Vanna White, Mary Hart, Rod Stewart's ex-wife Alana, Cornelia Guest, and fashion model Jennifer Flavin, but many more were lesser known "hyphenates" (model-actresses, artist-models, etc.).

It's possible Stallone was just being careful. Watching the scandal sheets over the last decade would be enough to frighten any star away from getting involved in more "stable" relationships. A person could get sued.

Lawsuits became vogue when actor Lee Marvin decided to marry his childhood sweetheart, Pamela Freeley, in May 1970. Marvin didn't take into account how singer-actress Michelle Triola, his live-in lover for the past six years, might feel when her monthly allowance checks suddenly stopped coming. She didn't like it and wasted no time in hiring show business lawyer Marvin Mitchelson to sue her lover for half of his income over those six years. Triola believed Marvin had taken responsibility for caring for her and that she had forfeited her career because of him. Mitchelson was hoping to prove that, although they had not been married, Triola was legally entitled to alimony, or, as the tabloids quickly put it, "palimony."

Above: William Hurt takes the witness stand to defend himself against Sandra Jennings' palimony suit. Opposite: Clint Eastwood and Sandra Locke make nice for the camera in Any Which Way You Can.

made even more grisly by the fact that the proceedings were televised and rebroadcast on nightly news programs.

The lawyer Jennings hired to help her get a piece of Hurt's earnings was Robert Golub, a flamboyant Manhattan attorney operating out of a five-story brownstone and flanked at all times by Mr. K, his turbaned Sikh manservant. Golub saw the case—win or lose—as a great publicity opportunity; he set out to capitalize on any witness or testimony that might turn the trial into a circus. It worked; each night viewers at home would tune in to see angry cross-fire testimony of Hurt, his ex-wife Mary Beth Hurt, his now ex-girlfriend Marlee Matlin, and Jennings, as Golub cross-examined each about Hurt's alleged physical abuse and alcoholic binges. In the end, Golub may have achieved his publicity goal, but he lost the case, failing to prove to the judge that his client and Hurt had ever said publicly that they were "married."

That same year, another suit was filed by Sandra Locke, live-in lover of Clint Eastwood. Eastwood and Locke met while costarring in *The Gauntlet*; Eastwood promptly left his wife for Locke, who was also married at the time. She was never divorced, and in fact, she and Eastwood bought a house for Locke's husband, who maintained a platonic relationship with Locke.

Locke said that once she had moved in with Eastwood, she assumed the duties of his wife for the next eleven years, during which time she had two abortions and a bilateral tubal ligation.

Then their relationship began to sour, and in April 1989, Eastwood (or one of his people) removed her belongings from the couple's luxurious Bel Air home while she was at work directing a feature. The locks were changed on the doors and a guard was posted outside the house. Locke, when notified on the set of Eastwood's actions, fainted.

In her suit, she claimed Eastwood had caused her "humiliation, mental anguish, severe emotional and physical distress." Dirty Harry, it seems, couldn't have been much dirtier. Obviously, all is fair in Hollywood dating games.

Eventually, a trial was held. Triola claimed Marvin's drinking was a factor in his ruining her career. Accounts were made of his holding a young woman out of a hotel window by her feet during a Las Vegas binge. The trial dragged on for twelve weeks. In the end, Triola was granted only $104,000—a fraction of the settlement she sued for. The judge refused to call the amount "alimony," saying instead that Triola should use the money to "rehabilitate" herself. As Marvin himself put it after the trial, the only real winner was Mitchelson, who proceeded to take on more cases for celebrity common-law wives, including Mrs. Nick Nolte and Mrs. Alice Cooper.

Perhaps the height of palimony ugliness was the bitter dispute between actor William Hurt and his former lover Sandra Jennings, all of which was

CHAPTER FIVE
Love and Marriage, More or Less

Star romances, no matter how casual or serious, never fail to make the gossip pages. But a star marriage can occasionally make history. From the days of Douglas Fairbanks and Mary Pickford, Hollywood's king and queen in the twenties, to the troubled on-again, off-again marriage of Sean Penn and Madonna, celebrity marriages have symbolized romance to us; the stars become our Romeo and Juliet, our Mark Antony and Cleopatra.

Although there were many notable star couples in Hollywood after sound came to the big screen, one couple's love affair rose above all others during the Golden Age of Hollywood in the thirties; indeed, their two names are synonymous with the purest romance: Clark Gable and Carole Lombard.

Clark Gable and Carole Lombard met several times before they began work on their first picture together, *No Man of Her Own*. But it was during that picture that their romance began. Gable, twenty-seven, was still married to his second wife, forty-five-year-old socialite Ria Langham. Gable had sought out women with experience from whom he could acquire the ambition, confidence, acting skill, and social graces he needed to make it as a star. These women taught him well and Gable was, at the time he met Lombard, the top romantic male lead in pictures.

Lombard had also been married twice: to actor William Powell and singer Russ Columbo. Columbo died in an accidental shooting at a friend's home, and Carole was one of the many people involved in helping convince Columbo's blind and very ill mother that he was alive and well, successfully touring Europe. Convinced that Mrs. Columbo was too frail to take the news of her son's death, Carole and the others kept up the charade until Mrs. Columbo died . . . eleven years later!

Gable and Lombard began to see each other in 1932, but were required to try and be as secretive as possible; Gable's second wife had refused to grant him a divorce. Gable and Lombard were described by friends as being the perfect couple. They thought she was just the right woman to stand up to this macho man, able to easily bring him back to earth or cut him down to size. When Gable was particularly full of himself over his film *Test Pilot*, she stood at the studio gate passing out handbills to employees urging them, if they wanted to see *really* bad acting, to be sure to catch Gable in *Parnell*, his biggest flop.

Eventually, Gable secured a divorce and the two planned to marry in 1939. Neither Gable nor Lombard wanted the marriage ceremony to be a public spectacle. Studio publicity people planned the wedding down to the last detail and in March 1939, Gable, Lombard, and a few very close friends rented some cars and drove to Kingman, Arizona. The elopement went off without a hitch. Once the happy couple returned to Hollywood, they sent out notices to each and every reporter, trying to show no favoritism. Louella Parsons, who felt she was a personal friend of the couple, became angry and retaliated; she did not include Gable in her annual list of her ten favorite stars—and this was the year that the epic *Gone With the Wind* was released.

Once they were married, the wild, extroverted Carole Lombard settled down a little. She spent fewer nights out on the town, bouncing from one fancy party to the next. She became more private, as Gable was; she even took up fishing and hunting and became a better shot than her husband.

With the coming of World War II, Gable was eager, like many people in Hollywood, to be a part of the action. He repeatedly asked President

Roosevelt how he might join the fight, but Roosevelt refused, saying he served a bigger purpose at home, entertaining the homefront, keeping up morale. Gable was unhappy with the president's position but finally accepted it when he convinced the president that he and Lombard might help sell war bonds. Together they took an active part in a massive bond drive.

Tragically, while returning from a bond drive tour in 1942, Carole Lombard was killed when the plane she was on crashed in the mountains between Nevada and California. Everyone on board died as well.

Opposite: Cary Grant and Katharine Hepburn take a walk down the aisle in **The Philadelphia Story.** *Above: Clark Gable and Carole Lombard arrive at the premiere of* **Gone With the Wind.**

> I can get a divorce whenever I want to. But my wife and Kate like things just as they are.
>
> —Spencer Tracy

Gable was devastated, and friends said that he never fully recovered from the blow. Shortly after his wife's death, Gable enlisted in the Air Force, flying dangerous missions over Germany. To some of the crew members who flew with him, Gable seemed to display "suicide courage"—a bravery they interpreted as an impulse to die in the war.

Gable survived, however, and went on to make more movies and to marry twice more. His first wife after Lombard was Lady Sylvia Ashley, the ex-wife of Douglas Fairbanks, Jr., whom he married near the end of a three-day drinking binge and who bore a striking physical similarity to Lombard. Ashley moved into the house Gable and Lombard had shared and was disturbed to find Gable kept the house exactly as it was with Lombard—and demanded that it stay that way. The new marriage lasted just sixteen months.

Later, after a period of dating various women in Hollywood, Gable married again, this time to another woman who resembled Lombard in physical appearance, Kay Williams Spreckels. It was with Spreckels that Gable sired his first and only child, a son. But Gable died before his son was born in 1962, shortly after the troubled and grueling filming of *The Misfits* with Marilyn Monroe.

Odds on favorites for king and queen of Hollywood in the forties might be Spencer Tracy and Katharine Hepburn, whose relationship became a symbol of Hollywood romance and the age-old battle of the sexes. Ironically, the pair never married.

In 1941, Hepburn enjoyed a triumphant return to Hollywood, where she accepted an Oscar for her performance in *The Philadelphia Story*. For her next project, she was set on doing *Woman of the Year* for MGM, and she had one actor in mind to play opposite her in the picture: Spencer Tracy.

Tracy and Hepburn had never met, and producer Joseph Mankiewicz arranged for them to do so. The meeting was prophetic. As he introduced the pair, Hepburn observed, "You're rather short, aren't you?" As Tracy stared back, working up a comeback, Mankiewicz peeled off, "Don't worry, honey. Before the picture is over, he'll cut you down to size."

Left: Katharine Hepburn and Spencer Tracy were a classic team both on and off the silver screen. Here they are in Adam's Rib.

Above: A scene from Guess Who's Coming to Dinner?, Hepburn and Tracy's last film together.

Though they seemed immediate adversaries, they agreed to make the picture, and once they began to work it was obvious they were becoming an "item." But this was an item like no other the town gossips had ever seen; for the first time, although everybody in Hollywood was talking about the relationship, no one raised an eyebrow or made a snide comment about it. Tracy and Hepburn were consummate professionals on the set, never letting their relationship get in the way of the work to be done. They were thus endeared to the crews (the source of most Hollywood dirt), and they commanded the respect of the press to the extent that reporters never blatantly questioned them about their relationship. Incredibly, the couple garnered all this respect despite the fact that Tracy was married and declined to ever divorce his wife.

Spencer Tracy and his wife, Louise, had been happily married at the start but became less so as Tracy's career took off. Together they had a son who was deaf, and they founded a clinic for deaf children. At one point in the early thirties, Tracy had an ill-fated affair with actress Loretta Young. His unhappiness at the time caused him to drink considerably, but once the affair had ended, he went back to Louise, who accepted him and forgot about the affair. These are the reasons, many believe, that Tracy could never bring himself to divorce Louise. He flatly denied his Catholicism kept him from divorce.

While Tracy was married and chose to keep his family together, Hepburn didn't mind at all. She had been married once, many years before, and knew that she was "not cut out for marriage"; in fact, she was staunchly independent. In this way they were nearly perfect for each other.

And so Tracy and Hepburn carried on their discreet romance, *never* showing any outward, public display of their affection, although it was well known that they had a deep love for each other. They worked well together on film, saw the world with a similar sense of humor, and constantly teased each other. Tracy had a long list of odd pet names for Hepburn—from Madame DeFarge to Coo-coo the Bird Girl.

Tracy's lifelong drinking problem took a toll on his kidneys and bladder, and his health began to seriously deteriorate. After attending his friend Clark Gable's 1960 funeral, Tracy was forced to stop working and rest. Hepburn, too, went into semiretirement for five years to nurse him.

In 1967, Hepburn and director Stanley Kramer coaxed Tracy to film *Guess Who's Coming to Dinner?* The studio's insurance company refused to insure the very ill Tracy on the picture, fearing he might not live to finish the project. In a little-known show of faith in his will to act again, Kramer and Hepburn put up their salaries on the film in lieu of insurance.

Tracy rallied his energy and dove into production, achieving great success; the film is considered by many to be his best work. But two weeks after shooting was completed, Spencer Tracy died from a heart attack while sitting at the kitchen table in the small cottage he shared with Hepburn. She was the one who found him.

There was another costar couple in the forties whose relationship has become a legend.

In 1944, director Howard Hawks was searching for an actress to play the female lead opposite Humphrey Bogart in his next film, an adaptation of Hemingway's *To Have and Have Not*. Hawks had no one particular in mind until he noticed the striking face of young Betty Perske on the cover of *Harper's Bazaar*. He immediately had her come to Hollywood for a screen test.

BACK TO THE ALTAR...

How many times have they been married?

Woody Allen	2
Julie Andrews	2
Fred Astaire	2
Lauren Bacall	2
Brigitte Bardot	3
John Barrymore	4
Ingrid Bergman	2
Humphrey Bogart	4
Ernest Borgnine	5
Marlon Brando	3
Yul Brynner	3
Raymond Burr	3
Ellen Burstyn	3
Richard Burton	5
Madeleine Carroll	4
Charlie Chaplin	4
Cher	2
Sean Connery	3
Joan Crawford	4
Bing Crosby	2
Tony Curtis	3
Bette Davis	4
Doris Day	4
Errol Flynn	3
Henry Fonda	4
Clark Gable	5
Ava Gardner	3
Judy Garland	5
Cary Grant	5
Oliver Hardy	2
Rex Harrison	6
Rita Hayworth	5
Audrey Hepburn	2
Katharine Hepburn	1
Rock Hudson	1

Above: Sparks fly between Humphrey Bogart and Lauren Bacall in Key Largo.

Her smoldering good looks and husky voice were perfect for the role, so Hawks introduced her to Bogart to get his approval. Bogart was very pleased with Hawks' choice, saying she looked "different," not like some woman out of a machine. He told her he was looking forward to acting with her. "I think we'll have some fun together," Bogart said.

Bogart, at age forty-five, was "fun" incarnate. The man was such a drinker, such a brawler, and such a "wencher" that he had a well-deserved bad reputation in Hollywood. It was a well-known fact that every day at 4:30 P.M., without fail, Bogart would take out a bottle of scotch and begin the night's drinking. He also was known for having terrible rows in public with his wife, Mayo Methot, that often came to physical blows; so common were these bouts, the couple was known as "the Battling Bogarts." Bogart's reputation was such that, upon being invited to a

Hollywood party, people would ask if Bogart would be there. If the answer was yes, the invitation was often politely declined.

But none of this bothered nineteen-year-old Betty Perske, now Lauren Bacall. She and Bogart began taking bicycle rides around the studio between shots, enjoying each other's company. Hawks noticed the chemistry and ordered the writers to put in more scenes between the two. Bogart's wife eventually got wind of the gossip about them and once angrily phoned the studio asking if "Mr. Bogart and his daughter" were available. *To Have and Have Not* was a great success, in no small part due to the incredible public curiosity about the love affair between its two magnetic stars.

Shortly after filming, Bogart was granted a divorce that prompted his distraught ex-wife to threaten suicide. Bogart returned to Methot long enough to talk her out of it.

Next to privacy, the rarest thing in Hollywood is a wedding anniversary.

—Gene Fowler

Bogart was finally happy in love but couldn't bring himself to marry Bacall, vacillating about their great age difference. Eventually she won him over completely and they were married on May 21, 1945, at Malabar, the Ohio farm of writer friend Louis Bromfield.

Bacall, or Baby, as Bogart called her, was good for him. Friends noticed that once they were married, he drank considerably less (although he didn't stop completely); he brawled less; and he womanized *far* less. That's not to say Bogart and Bacall lived a sedate lifestyle; on the contrary, they were part of a group of Hollywood people who lived life for the moment; they would troop off to Las Vegas for days on end, gambling, drinking, and enjoying themselves with a tight-knit group of friends that included Frank Sinatra, Dean Martin, and Sammy Davis, Jr. Bacall once stood looking at the entourage, near the end of just such a binge, and said, "You look like a goddamned rat pack." The name stuck and the group was known as the "rat pack" for years. Sinatra went on to use the name for another group of show-business party boys in Las Vegas in the sixties.

Bogart and Bacall had two children, Stephen and Leslie (named after their friend Leslie Howard) and they made three more well-received films together: *The Big Sleep*; *Key Largo*; and *Dark Passage*.

In 1956, Bogart was diagnosed with esophagus cancer. He underwent a grueling eight-hour operation that nearly killed him but was called "successful." The thin, frail actor continued to smoke and drink; Bacall even helped pour his liquor, knowing Bogart wanted to live life as he

Right: Bogey, Bacall, and their son, Stephen, at their Los Angeles home, 1952.

Below: Orson Welles paints the town with the object of his desire, Rita Hayworth.

chose and no other way. Less than a year later, on January 14, 1957, Bogart said, "Goodbye, Kid," as he went to bed. He died in his sleep.

Gable and Lombard, Tracy and Hepburn, Bogey and Bacall—these names are synonymous with romance in the thirties and forties and they even have an idyllic ring today. But love didn't come so easy to other Hollywood stars.

Take Rita Hayworth, for example—a woman who symbolized romance and sex, who was considered a "goddess of love." Her external beauty was essentially manufactured by Columbia Pictures—they raised her hairline and eyebrows and reshaped her figure through diet—yet she remained her pre-Hollywood self, the insecure, virtually uneducated Margarita Cansino, who spent her childhood dancing in nightclubs with her abusive father. Hayworth seemed to have it all—good looks, a thriving movie career, and relationships with some of the most famous men in the world—but love was a confusing, hurtful part of her life, and she was at constant odds with her love goddess image.

Orson Welles was not even thirty years old when he

was hailed as a "genius" for frightening audiences with his "War of the Worlds" broadcast and reaching a highwater mark in film excellence with *Citizen Kane*. This brilliant young intellectual saw a photo of Rita Hayworth in *Life* magazine while on location in South America; he was so taken with the sultry pinup—the beautiful Hayworth clad only in a slip, curled up on satin sheets—that he vowed to marry her when he got back to Hollywood.

Upon his return, he began to speak openly about how she would be his wife. Word eventually reached the insecure Hayworth, who quickly assumed that the intellectual filmmaker was making fun of her.

Welles arranged a party at which to meet her and was immediately taken with her "sweetness" and what he considered her non–movie star quality. But even after meeting Welles, Hayworth continued to rebuff him. Her refusal to take the obsessed man's calls only strengthened his persistence; he called her home continuously for five weeks until she finally took his call. When she did, they made plans to go out that night.

> If I found a man who had $15 million, would sign over half of it to me before the marriage, and guarantee he'd be dead within a year.
>
> — Bette Davis, when asked if she would marry again

Almost immediately Welles tuned into her incredible insecurity and neurotic jealousy. He convinced her to marry him and later said that he did so to help her. "That's why I married her," he said, "I adored her. It *had* to be done for her."

For Hayworth, Welles was the answer to her prayers. He had designs on a career in politics and promised to take her away from Hollywood, where she was miserable in her life as a star under Harry Cohn's wrath. She became pregnant and what she needed seemed finally within reach—a normal family life with her husband and child.

Welles, however, was uninterested in children and when his political career faltered, he was forced back to Hollywood to act for a living. He became despondent, having frequent affairs—including one with Judy Garland—and even sought solace with prostitutes. The marriage fell apart; Hayworth's relationship with the man whom she would always consider her one great love was over. She was granted a divorce in November, 1947.

Hayworth had romances with several men after her divorce from Welles, including an affair with Howard Hughes; she became pregnant by him, but quietly terminated the pregnancy. Then, in quick succession, she suffered the death of her mother and a falling out with Columbia studios, specifically with Harry Cohn. Hayworth set off for Europe in the summer of 1948 to take a much-needed vacation from the emotional beating she'd taken over the last few years. And it was in Europe, on the Mediterranean, where she not only met the man who would be her next husband, but entered into one of the most public romances in history.

While Rita vacationed in Cannes, she caught the eye of the Moslem Prince Aly Kahn at a party. The rich and charming prince had been with literally hundreds of women in his life, but he always found time for new encounters. When he saw the tall, beautiful American actress, he fell instantly in love—perhaps with her screen image—and began his campaign to win her over. The prince

Left: Prince Aly Kahn and his new bride, Rita Hayworth, head home after their civil marriage ceremony.

sent three dozen roses to her the next morning and every morning thereafter while she stayed in Cannes; he telephoned her constantly; and he stationed a car and driver outside her hotel so that she could come to him instantly should the mood strike her. Kahn became convinced his lavishly decorated Riviera palace wasn't up to par and had it completely redone, installing new furniture, drapes, dishes, and linens. The prince brought in a new chef, one who was expert at American cooking.

Slowly, Rita came out of her depression, partly through the flurry of attention she was getting in Cannes. The Prince had a lot of competition for her affections, including the Shah of Iran. Eventually Kahn won out, and after that, he and Hayworth were inseparable. They lived a true jet-set lifestyle, going off to Rome for lunch, to Paris or London for dinner and a show. One particularly trying day, the couple took off for Lisbon, but their arrival caused a near riot; to avoid the chaos, they took off for Biarritz, and as

A SIMPLE HOLLYWOOD WEDDING

In 1988, Michael J. Fox planned to marry actress Tracy Pollan in a small, private ceremony at the West Mountain Inn in Arlington, Vermont. As Fox later reported, that simple wish was the equivalent of "throwing down the gauntlet" to the gossip press, whose elaborate attempts at "getting the story" turned the Hollywood couple's modest, intimate ceremony into a fiasco.

Fox contacted Gavin de Becker, renowned celebrity security specialist, to handle security for the wedding. De Becker mapped out the surrounding area, set up checkpoints on area roads and bridges, "designed a traffic-control and credential system," and modified three vehicles with tinted windows, two-way radios, and special lights. The bride and groom were code-named "the coyotes," and the press "the paperboys."

Tabloid activity increased as the big day grew near, with reporters casing out the bride's New York apartment and impersonating Fox's father in an attempt to get details from florists and caterers. One reporter even went so far as to pose as a local tour guide, offering to take the bride's grandparents out "sight-seeing" . . . and to pump them for information. De Becker countered by placing Fox's press agent, Nancy Rider, undercover in the offices of the *National Enquirer*'s command center in a nearby town, posing as a temporary office worker. This way he knew every move the tabloid people made.

On the wedding day, the "paperboys" were out in full force—six helicopters hovered noisily overhead and dozens of camouflaged photographers swarmed through the surrounding woods. The security forces were successful; no photographs of the actual wedding were released until the couple did so themselves, except for one shot of the honeymooners wading in the ocean in their swimsuits a few days later. That shot was snapped by a photographer in a scuba suit who swam up and surfaced near the two with a waterproof camera.

the plane landed, they were again surrounded by a mass of screaming fans; so they turned around and returned to Cannes.

After four months of fun with Kahn, Hayworth got cold feet, fearing another major involvement, and returned to Hollywood. Shortly thereafter Kahn moved into a home around the corner from hers to continue his pursuit.

Kahn was still legally married the time, and while the two lovers jetted around the world in search of privacy, public sentiment over the affair grew to a boil. London papers decried "This affair is an insult to all decent women!" The *Hollywood Reporter* suggested, "the motion picture industry should wash its hands of Rita Hayworth."

Eventually Kahn was granted a divorce, and in May 1949, he and Hayworth were married—in two separate ceremonies. The first was a city hall ceremony for ninety of the world's most exclusive guests (including Louella Parsons, of course), and the next day they were married again in a private Moslem ceremony (to appease Moslems who might someday be Princess Rita's subjects).

Almost immediately after marrying, the differences between the two became apparent. Battle lines were drawn. Hayworth hated her Hollywood image, wanted to wear jeans, and lay around the palace eating candy. She let the bright red dye grow out of her hair, preferring its natural dark brown color. Kahn wanted to go out every night, to show off his movie-star bride.

Rita gave birth to Princess Yasmin a short seven months after the wedding. Soon after, Harry Cohn paid a visit to the palace where he pleaded with Hayworth to return to work. "Princesses don't act in movies," she told him. But things weren't working out with Kahn. Eventually, Hayworth wanted a divorce. Kahn refused. Fearing child custody problems associated with the Islamic religion, Hayworth escaped under cover of the night with Yasmin; she slipped out of the palace and, under an assumed name, snuck aboard a vessel bound for the United States.

Hayworth briefly stayed in New York as divorce proceedings began. When the divorce was final, she headed out West. Upon arrival in Hollywood, she signed on with Cohn at Columbia.

Kahn soon followed Hayworth back to the United States and pleaded with her to return. She went back to Europe to give the marriage another chance, but immediately realized that the situation was hopeless. She returned within a week, no longer Princess Rita.

During the conservative fifties, movie fans were hard-pressed to find full-tilt romances to keep them riveted to the gossip pages, especially once Debbie Reynolds and Eddie Fisher settled down into boring wedded bliss (at least, that's what it looked like). And so fans were desperate for dirt when it became known that Natalie Wood and Robert Wagner were seeing each other.

Opposite: Natalie Wood, leading ingenue of the fifties.

Natalie Wood was a child star who managed to parlay her childhood fame into a career as a near-adult to become one of the leading ingenues of the fifties. Wood had been introduced to Wagner, who was eight years her senior, just before she began dating Elvis Presley. Fans thought things between Wood and the King of Rock and Roll were heating up as Wood flew to Memphis to meet Presley's family, but the romance wasn't to be. Natalie cut the trip short and returned to Hollywood; she said Presley was "good at singing, but not much else" and expressed disappointment with his clean lifestyle—drinking, smoking, and swearing were noticeably absent.

Upon her return to Hollywood, she received a call from Wagner asking her if she was done fooling around with "that creep" Presley and ready to go out with him. She agreed, and he invited her out on his boat, *My Lady*. She spent the night on the boat. Soon the two were the next hot romantic item.

Looking back, insiders say that the whirl of publicity surrounding the two probably saved them both from sliding into obscurity like many of their contemporaries—forgotten names like Ty Hardin, Lori Nelson, John Smith, and Diane Varsi.

The press attention focused on Wagner and Wood was so great that they were forced to elope, stealing away to Scottsdale, Arizona, where they locked and barred the church doors behind them to ensure absolute privacy. Nonetheless, photographs of the wedding appeared in fan magazines almost immediately—a "friend" they'd invited snapped the photos and sold them to the fan rags for $10,000. It was the beginning of the couple's lifelong belligerent attitude toward the press.

Natalie was beginning to worry about her career, having landed few parts of any merit since her role in *Rebel Without a Cause*. Her fears were allayed when she was cast opposite Warren Beatty in *Splendor in the Grass*. Wagner was not so happy, knowing full well Beatty's reputation as a womanizer. Wagner made his presence known on the set each day, staying by Wood's side and

Below: Natalie Wood and Robert Wagner, happy together once again, in 1981.

watching Beatty like a hawk. Everyone expected Beatty to make a move, and even the crew was surprised that nothing seemed to come of the volatile situation.

But soon after the picture had wrapped, Beatty struck, calling Wood on the phone and working his charm. Even though it was not in her nature to be unfaithful, she fell for Beatty's line; as a friend of Beatty's once said, "Warren in heat is irresistible."

Wood and Beatty began an affair which eventually became public knowledge, and three years after their private wedding in Arizona, Wood and Wagner were divorced. Elizabeth Taylor, who believed very strongly in Wood and Wagner's love, was so upset by the break she swallowed several sedatives and took to her bed. Wagner, stung by the divorce, his career on the wane, took off for Europe.

Wood's relationship with Beatty came to an ugly close a little over a year later. The two were dining at Chasen's, a posh Beverly Hills eatery frequented by Hollywood's elite; dining nearby

were Mr. and Mrs. Alfred Hitchcock, Mr. and Mrs. James Stewart, and Mr. and Mrs. Gregory Peck. Midway through the meal Beatty excused himself to go to the men's room; Wood waited patiently for him to return.

He never did.

Instead of visiting the men's room, Beatty ditched Wood and propositioned a voluptuous coat-check girl. They snuck out of the restaurant together and took off on a three-day revel.

When Beatty returned to Wood's home a week later to pick up his belongings (after the ugly scene had been reported in the press), he found that she had tossed everything into the incinerator.

Wagner and Wood spent the rest of the sixties apart. Each married again, Wagner to Marion Marshall, whom he'd befriended while working in Rome, and Wood to English talent agent Richard Gregson. Neither marriage lasted, and when Wood was separated from Gregson in 1972, she and "R.J." were seen dating again. They attended the 1972 Academy Award presentations together; their arrival drew more attention than the return of Charlie Chaplin to Hollywood to accept an honorary award after a thirty-six-year exile in Europe.

They were married that year—again, in secret—in a ceremony aboard Wagner's yacht *Ramblin' Rose*. Afterward they quickly settled into their roles as Hollywood's dream couple. Wagner pursued a very successful television career, moving from one hit series to the next, on shows like *It Takes a Thief*, *Switch*, and *Hart to Hart*. Natalie chose to focus on being a mother and accepted far fewer acting jobs. The couple lived happily this way, steadfastly in love, until Wood's tragic drowning in November 1981. Ironically, theirs was a romance that began and sadly ended aboard a yacht at sea. (For details on the tragedy, see page 154.)

Natalie Wood's untimely death brought an end to a solid marriage between two people who were finally ready to dedicate themselves to each other. Fortunately, another Hollywood couple, Joanne Woodward and Paul Newman,

> The trouble with marrying an actor is they grab you in their arms, hold you close and tell you how wonderful they are.
>
> —Shelley Winters

Left: Paul Newman and Joanne Woodward in their Beverly Hills home, 1958.

didn't have to wait nearly as long as Wood and Wagner to settle into a marriage that would last. Married around the same time as Wagner and Wood, Newman and Woodward have remained married to each other—exclusively—for over thirty years, a remarkable achievement for a show business marriage.

Woodward and Newman met when both were struggling young actors making the rounds of New York City theatrical agents in the fifties. They became friends and were cast together in a 1952 Broadway production of *Picnic*. At the time, Newman was married, and his wife, Jacqueline, was expecting a second child, so he fought off his feelings for Woodward while working beside her every night. Eventually, the two actors went their separate ways.

In 1954, Newman was awarded a contract with Warners. He sent his wife and children to live with her family in Wisconsin and headed out to Hollywood, where Joanne Woodward happened to be working under contract to Twentieth Century-Fox. Newman's feelings for Woodward flared up again, and he found himself in a painful dilemma, trying to choose between his wife and children and Woodward. He began drinking heavily to try and drown out his feelings. Although his star was rising at the time, he claims this was the most unhappy period of his life.

Newman sought analysis and eventually worked up the courage to ask his wife for a divorce. She refused. Paul persisted, and after making *The Long Hot Summer* in 1958, he made his way to Mexico where he eventually received a divorce. In January 1958, he and Woodward were married in Las Vegas; a year later she had their first child. Woodward promptly hired a nursemaid and returned to work, filming *The Fugitive Kind* and beginning a lifelong struggle of seesawing between her career and motherhood.

Meanwhile, Newman's first son, Scott, had developed into a troubled young man, greatly disturbed by the differences between his father's successful lifestyle and that of his mother, Jacqueline. In 1975, after a long battle with drug addiction, Scott died of an overdose; the trauma turned Newman and Woodward on a philanthropic course. Together the couple formed the Scott Newman Foundation to help young drug addicts. Newman also developed a line of food products, Newman's Own, directing the profits to various charities.

Through both the good and bad times, Woodward and Newman have stuck together, proving that a star marriage doesn't necessarily have to be fraught with constant troubles and separations. But, then again, that's just one couple. An entirely different picture of celebrity marriage emerges when the complex love life of Elizabeth Taylor is unraveled. She alone is responsible for eight of the highest-profile marriages in Hollywood history.

Taylor's first husband was the young Nicky Hilton, son of the chairman of the Hilton Hotel chain, whom she met in a nightclub in late 1950. The two were engaged in February 1951 and married by May. She was nineteen years old.

MGM was pleased with Taylor's engagement at the time, as they were preparing the release of her latest picture, *Father of the Bride*, and saw a chance for the wedding to coincide with the release date. The studio financed the entire wedding, knowing the publicity involved would be well worth the investment—or so they hoped.

By the time the two young people returned from their honeymoon in Europe, it was clear they were not meant for each other. They argued almost constantly, and Hilton revealed a wicked temper; the honeymoon—and the marriage—was over in two short months.

Taylor didn't have to wait long for another chance. In 1952, the twenty-year-old actress met and fell in love with Michael Wilding, an unimposing, forty-year-old English actor she began dating while filming *Ivanhoe* in London.

Wilding left behind a twenty-year contract to a studio in England and headed for Hollywood and his new bride, Taylor. But upon his arrival in the American movie capital, it was obvious he was a fish out of water; a friend described him as "far too casual and unambitious a

involved in a horrible automobile accident. Taylor ran to the scene of the accident and cradled Clift's bloodied head until the ambulance arrived. And it was while nursing her friend Clift back to health that she met producer Mike Todd.

Taylor and Todd were a couple almost instantly, and the attraction was powerful; shortly after they began dating, Todd declared to Taylor, "from now on, you will f— nobody but me."

Todd was gruff and crude and often fondled Taylor's breasts in public, but he loved her and was responsible for getting her away from the studio and a flat domestic situation. He also thrust her into the limelight as an international star.

They were married in 1957. Eddie Fisher, Todd's best friend, was the best man; Debbie Reynolds, Fisher's wife, was matron of honor.

Todd worked hard for Taylor, landing her one of the best roles of her career, Maggie in *Cat on a Hot Tin Roof*, opposite Paul Newman. Two weeks into the shooting of *Cat*, Taylor got word that Todd had died in a fiery plane crash en route to New York. Taylor was devastated, as much by Todd's death as by the funeral fiasco—photographers mobbed her and fans begged the grieving widow for her autograph.

Liz Taylor's first three husbands. Opposite: Liz with Nick Hilton. Left: With Michael Wilding in London. Below: With Mike Todd and two-year-old Christopher at the London premiere of **Around the World in Eighty Days.**

figure to succeed in the Hollywood machine." He spent most of his time on suspension from the meager contract he managed to get, lounging around the house and watching the children. Taylor admitted years later that, although she'd been with Wilding for five years and had two children by him, it was almost impossible to remember being married to him at all. He was that boring.

Taylor went off to jump-start her career with her role in *Giant* and met James Dean. While she and Dean did not become romantically involved, he introduced her to a new lifestyle, one that was far removed from her very stale marriage to Wilding. Taylor and Wilding essentially separated, yet continued to live together in the same Hollywood house.

It was this house that Taylor's close friend, Montgomery Clift, was leaving when he was

She is famine, fire, destruction and plague; she is the Dark Lady of the Sonnets... She is a secret wrapped in an enigma inside a mystery.

— Richard Burton,
on his wife
Elizabeth
Taylor

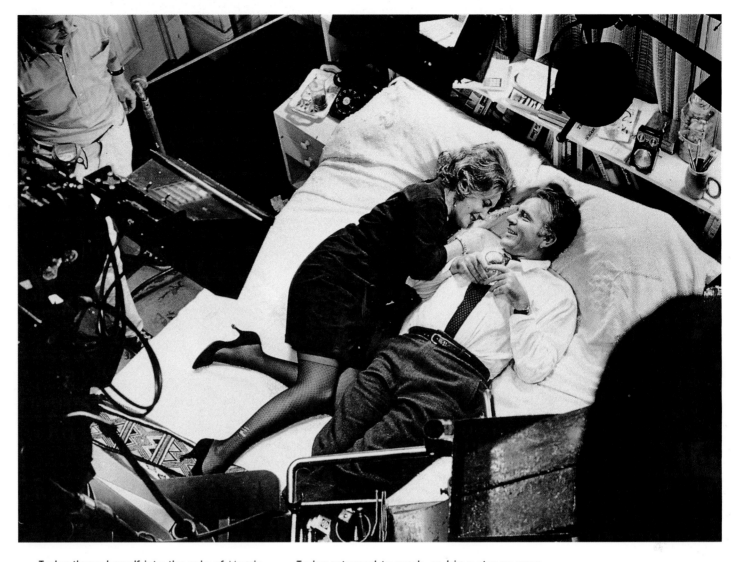

Taylor threw herself into the role of Maggie, shutting down when she wasn't on camera and coming to life only to act. She also found solace in the company of Todd's good friend, Eddie Fisher. Soon they were dating; they had a tryst in the Catskills during his summer cabaret. A frenzy of outrage resulted: here was Taylor, dating a happily married man (not true), her late husband's best friend, a mere six months after his death! Hedda Hopper intoned, "America will never forgive you."

The Taylor-Fisher scandal was balanced out by the tremendous success of *Cat on a Hot Tin Roof*; for every person in America who believed her behavior was scandalous, another found her activities acceptable, perhaps even titillating. She and Fisher were married in May 1959, and Taylor hoped to retire from films, but Fisher, it turned out, wasn't enough of a success to support them.

Taylor returned to work, as big a star as ever, while Fisher's popularity seemed to wane, his name a national joke, forever linked with what *not* to do when one's husband is killed. Jacqueline Kennedy, a few years after her husband's assassination, cracked, "the public will never turn against me. Unless of course I marry Eddie Fisher."

While in England, shooting the big-budget epic *Cleopatra*, Taylor was stricken with a life-threatening attack of lung congestion. The world watched her recovery, and the press, posting daily reports on her health, became more benevolent to her cause, less prurient in its coverage of her life.

While Taylor recovered, the multimillion dollar fiasco *Cleopatra* was rewritten and recast. The role of Mark Antony went to a classical stage actor, Richard Burton.

They say marriages are made in heaven. So are thunder and lightning.

— Clint Eastwood

The picture, already rumored to be tens of millions of dollars over budget after its move from England to Rome, was closely watched by the media and constantly surrounded with paparazzi. Stories began to circulate about a sizzling behind-the-scenes romance between Taylor and her leading man, Burton.

Eddie Fisher called a press conference in New York to deny any rumors of marital problems. To make his point, he called Taylor on the set in Rome and asked her to confirm, over the phone and to the press, that nothing was going on. "Well, Eddie, I can't actually do that," she replied, "because there is, you see, some truth in the rumors."

The two actors playing the world's best-known lovers in the world's most expensive movie ever made were having an affair. The entire mess became known to those close to Burton and Taylor as *le scandale*.

During the year it took to edit *Cleopatra* down to size, Burton and Taylor were each granted a divorce and made a film together (*The V.I.P.'s*). They were married in 1964.

At first, the couple could do no wrong. They were the screen's greatest couple, appearing successfully in *Who's Afraid of Virginia Woolf?* and *The Taming of the Shrew*. Burton showered Taylor with gifts, including the 69.42 carat Cartier-Burton diamond, her most prized piece of jewelry. But eventually, the two began to fall from grace; fans, uninterested in happy couples, looked elsewhere for gossipy excitement.

Taylor and Burton's initial successes were followed by a long string of box-office bombs. They reached a sad low in 1970, appearing on *The Lucille Ball Show* in a gaudy parody of themselves. Burton began drinking heavily and having affairs. Finally, after releasing a dreary television drama called, of all things, *Divorce His—Divorce Hers*, in 1973, they separated. A short time later, they were divorced.

But not for long. Within a year the two were seen together again and were married a second time in October 1975. As Taylor put it, they were "joined at the hip" and had no choice.

Burton had dried out during the divorce and separation. Now, back with Taylor, he was back on the bottle. He fell in love with Susan Hunt, a neighbor to their Swiss chalet and, once again, he and Taylor were divorced.

Taylor met her seventh husband, John Warner, at a Bicentennial dinner in July 1976. At the time, she was not in demand for either movies or television, and so she settled for a career as a political wife. By Christmas she had married Warner and taken up helping him run for

Above: Liz at a press conference for her latest perfume, White Diamonds, with her eighth husband, ex-Teamster Larry Fortensky, 1990.

the Senate. For two years she did virtually nothing but campaign for her husband and gain a tremendous amount of weight. In 1979 he was elected and sent to Capitol Hill; once there, Taylor found Washington life extremely dull. While Warner worked away in his office she was left to sit and watch television. She decided to return to acting, coming back via Broadway in a revival of *The Little Foxes* in 1982.

Taylor had rediscovered acting, and she divorced Warner that same year. But she had developed a lot of bad habits. Now grossly bloated, Taylor lived day to day on a stream of pills and alcohol. She checked herself into the Betty Ford Clinic; there found a fit and healthy body and mind as well as a new philosophy for living: "lone survival from within."

For the next few years, Taylor held fast to her new single, clean, and sober outlook on life, and even broke engagements to two wealthy men—Mexican attorney Victor Luna in 1984 and businessman Dennis Stein in 1985—to make sure she stayed that way.

But by 1988, following a bad back injury and the death of two close friends, Malcolm Forbes and Halston, she was back on drugs. In the autumn of that year she once again checked into the Betty Ford Clinic, where she gained control over her substance abuse. There she also found peace of mind—and her latest love, Larry Fortensky.

Taylor met the divorced Teamster, who happens to be twenty-three years her junior, in group therapy sessions at the clinic. Their attraction was immediate and since leaving the clinic together that year, they have rarely been seen apart. Taylor attended the funeral of Fortensky's mother, and he was at Taylor's side during her near-fatal bout with pneumonia in 1990.

In August 1991, Taylor announced their engagement. In October the couple was married on the grounds of "Neverland," singer Michael Jackson's ranch near Santa Barbara, California. Although Fortensky is no Hollywood star, the wedding, Taylor's eighth, did not fail to live up to expectations. Jackson, a close friend of Taylor's,

walked the bride down the aisle and gave her away, while a dozen tabloid-chartered helicopters hovered noisily overhead, all but drowning out the couple's nuptials.

After announcing plans for her eighth high-profile marriage, Elizabeth Taylor told the *Hollywood Reporter*, "I always said I would get married one more time, and with God's blessings, this is it, forever." Can glamorous Elizabeth Taylor find true, lasting love with a guy who drives a Caterpillar dirt compactor for a living? Only time will tell.

With Elizabeth Taylor taking nearly ten years between marriages, the 1980s might have been a drab time for fans who wanted some juicy Hollywood marital gossip. But thanks to pop singing sensation/movie star Madonna and her bumpy life with temperamental Method actor Sean Penn, fans weren't disappointed.

The two met on the set of Madonna's "Material Girl" video in February 1985. As *People* magazine put it, he was "art," an actor who dressed in jeans and searched his soul to bring characters "on the edge" to life in "important" films, and she was "commerce," a pop-music

Below: Sean Penn and Madonna, in happier times, taking a stroll in New York City.

superstar who happened to squeak and shake her way through a series of silly Hollywood movies. But somehow, they were drawn to each other and by August of that year they were married in a private ceremony in Malibu as tabloid photographers in helicopters whirled noisily and obtrusively overhead.

Almost immediately Madonna became concerned about Penn's infamous drinking and violent outbursts; she was quick to seek psychiatric help and tried in vain to convince Penn to get some as well. He refused.

In April 1986, Penn spotted Madonna in a Los Angeles nightclub talking with her old friend, songwriter David Wolinski. Penn suspected Wolinski was moving in on his wife, flew into a rage, and attacked the man with his fists, feet, and a chair. Penn was arrested, fined $1,000, and given a year's probation.

It became clear that Penn was obsessively jealous, believing Madonna was having an affair with every man she came in contact with. He continued his violent behavior, punching anyone who tried to snap his picture, getting pulled over for drunk driving in Los Angeles, both behaviors in violation of his probation. He was given a sixty-day jail term. He only served thirty-three days, getting an early release, ironically, for good behavior.

Not long after Penn's September 1987 release from jail, Madonna served him with divorce papers. It looked like the brief and violent marriage was at an end. But thirteen days later the two announced a reconciliation.

The next year was a relatively quiet one. Penn seemed as if he wanted to make the marriage work and moved a production of the play *Hurlyburly* from New York to Los Angeles in order to be closer to his wife. Madonna started spending a great deal of time with comedienne Sandra Bernhard; the two made a provocative appearance together on *Late Night with David Letterman*; dressed alike, they fondled each other while giggling about being "just friends."

On opening night for *Hurlyburly* in Los Angeles, Madonna arrived late—and with Bernhard at her side. Later, at the opening night celebration in Century City, Penn lost his cool about the situation and screamed into her face, "How could you do this to me?"

Two months later, in December 1988, the police were called to investigate a domestic violence call at the couple's Malibu home. Rumors swirled around Hollywood that Sean strapped Madonna to a chair and whipped her. Madonna filed assault charges but later dropped them. This time, however, when divorce papers were drawn up, the separation was final.

Why do Hollywood divorces cost so much? Because they're worth it.

—Johnny Carson

Left: Julia Roberts with costar and then-fiancé Kiefer Sutherland in Flatliners, *1990.*

The two Hollywood dynamos have each gone their separate ways. Madonna has since been linked with several big stars, most notably Warren Beatty, and she escorted Michael Jackson to the 1991 Oscar ceremony. Still, she continues to publicly profess her love for Sean. Penn has reportedly calmed down some; he has managed to keep out of the tabloids lately and has had a child with actress Robin Wright.

And round and round it goes. Julia Roberts, one of the current queens of Hollywood, literally rocketed to stardom overnight. As recently as 1987, she appeared in her first feature film, a straight-to-video western called *Blood Red*. By 1991 she was the highest-paid female star in the business—all this and an Academy Award nomination for her role in *Steel Magnolias*—by the tender age of twenty-three. Everyone loves Julia Roberts, and there was plenty of tabloid excite-

ment about her coming 1991 marriage to Kiefer Sutherland, the brat-pack son of Donald Sutherland (a star in his own right) and Julia's costar in the thriller *Flatliners*.

But scant hours before the scheduled ceremony on a soundstage at Fox Studios, Julia asked that the scores of guests (including her family and many of Hollywood's "A" list) be contacted and told the wedding was off. Was it because of Kiefer's late-night carousing with a stripper? Sources close to both parties say the troubles ran deeper than that. Whatever the reason, Julia left for Ireland the next day with her close friend, actor Jason Patric, while Sutherland retreated to the home of his ex-wife. The press and fans went wild over the news. And so ended the latest play, fervently watched by adoring fans on the sidelines, in one of our favorite spectator sports: movie-star matrimony.

Sin City

part three

City

CHAPTER SIX

Land O' Excess and Abuse

After World War I, the sudden riches reaped by Hollywood's movie stars and moguls (which were taxed very little, if at all) were enough to send any small industrial community over the brink; excess became the rule of the day. The stars built bigger and bigger homes. Just when Gloria Swanson's showplace seemed to take the prize, Douglas Fairbanks and Mary Pickford built their grand Tudor palace, Pickfair. Not to be outdone, Harold Lloyd, comedy king of the silents, topped them all with his sixteen-acre (6.5-ha) Beverly Hills estate, Greenacres. From 1924 to 1928, Lloyd built his dream estate, indulging every whim at an incredible cost for those times—$2.5 million. The result was a forty-four-room Italian Renaissance palace, surrounded by an English cottage, floral gardens, an Olympic-size swimming pool, and a private lagoon.

Cars, too, were part of the grand game of one-upmanship. The talk of the town was comedian Fatty Arbuckle's custom-built $25,000 Rolls-Royce, complete with a working toilet in the backseat. Clark Gable topped rival Gary Cooper by ordering a custom-made Dussenberg that was a foot (30 cm) longer than Cooper's model. But Harold Lloyd won this contest hands down as well, tooling around town in a thirty-foot (9-m) yacht on wheels, complete with portholes, a galley, and a foghorn.

Opulence was but one spoke in the wheel of Hollywood excess. Most integral to life in Tinseltown were fast living and drug use (today called drug abuse).

The drug of choice in Hollywood during the roaring twenties was cocaine. Its use was so widespread, the drug has been cited as an influence on the manic movie style of the period, the best-known example of which might be the leaping, frenetic Keystone Kops.

The theory might not be far off base; cocaine at the time was all-pervasive. In 1922, at the peak of Hollywood's no-holds-barred debauchery, *Vanity Fair* magazine printed this short description of a party in Hollywood:

> Last week little Lulu Lenore of the Cuckoo Comedy Co. gave a small house dance for the younger addicts. 'Will you come to my "Snow"-ball' read the clever invitations. In one corner of the living room was a miniature 'drug-store,' where Otho Everhard kept the company in a roar as he dispensed little packages of cocaine, morphine and heroin. The guests, at their departure, received exquisite hypodermic needles in vanity boxes which have caused many heart-burnings among those not invited.

Despite this open attitude toward addiction, Hollywood managed to keep the general public in the dark concerning its wicked ways, until a long, ugly string of scandals drew national attention to the insular community. These included a scandal surrounding America's best-loved actor at the time, Wallace Reid.

In March 1922, Reid checked into Banksia Place Sanitarium to cure his overpowering morphine addiction. The revelation of Reid's drug addiction was instantly front-page news and a big blow to the public, which responded with a great outpouring of sympathy for the stricken actor. But sympathy turned to shock when Reid died in the sanitarium less than a year later. His wife claimed that "only a return to the drug under control could have saved him. He refused."

Had he survived, there is some doubt that Reid would have had a career to return to. Studio moguls and the infamous Hays Office they cre-

ated to monitor their industry, had compiled a document called "The Doom Book"—a list of 117 Hollywood figures who were known drug users or addicts and marked to be blacklisted; Reid's name was in "The Doom Book."

The campaign against drugs was massive, and even Reid's widow tried to carry the message; taking her story to the people, she traveled across the country for years, talking about the evils of drug addiction to anyone who would listen. (She appeared, billed as "Mrs. Wallace Reid," in an antidrug film called *Human Wreckage*.) The first of the Hollywood witch-

Opposite: A scene from **The Four Horsemen of the Apocalypse**, *1921.* *Above: Tallulah Bankhead, a flapper fond of cocaine, or as it was commonly dubbed, "joy powder."*

hunts was on. Careers were ruined. Drug users were forced to exercise more caution and were effectively driven underground.

But "The Doom Book" was also notable for its blatant omissions. Tallulah Bankhead, another flapper fond of "joy powder," managed to flourish as a star for forty years, despite her legendary cocaine-induced behavior at parties. A friend of Bankhead's, actress Estelle Winwood recalled that Tallulah would begin every evening as a "piquant little match girl," sitting quietly or showing photographs of her mother, but as time passed and she snorted more cocaine, she began doing cartwheels in the center of the room. "When the cartwheels . . . ceased to amuse or shock," Winwood said, "Tallulah took to doing them without any underwear on."

Even the most drug-crazed of all twenties starlets, the "too beautiful" Barbara LaMarr, managed to avoid inclusion in "The Doom Book," despite the fact that she went through six husbands, innumerable lovers, and "vast quantities" of heroin, opium, morphine, and cocaine that she kept in a solid gold casket atop her piano. Managing to stay off the "list" did her no good, however; she died from a suicidal overdose at the age of twenty-six.

While the truly seedy side of Hollywood's excessiveness was pushed further and further underground, its megalomania and eccentricity flourished as it never had before during the thirties and forties.

Pickfair had been the social center for Hollywood in the twenties, but in the thirties its owners, Mary Pickford and Douglas Fairbanks, divorced. The void they left was filled by newspaper tycoon William Randolph Hearst and his longtime mistress Marion Davies; the couple played host to Hollywood's elite in Hearst's massive home, San Simeon, north of Santa Barbara.

I'm no alcoholic. I'm a drunkard. There's a difference. A drunkard doesn't like to go to meetings.

—Jackie
Gleason

Right: Marion Davies counts her blessings at San Simeon—the Hearst Castle—circa 1932.

What do you want me to do, stop shooting and release it as The Five Command-ments?

—Cecil B. De Mille, on charges of overspending

(The tremendous castle was under constant construction, as Hearst believed that if he stopped building he would die.)

Each weekend, forty or fifty of the most important people in Hollywood boarded Hearst's special railroad cars and were taken north to San Luis Obispo, where a fleet of limousines would transport the guests up to the damp, drafty castle on the hill. The gourmet multicourse meals were served at a fifty-four-foot (16-m) seventeenth-century wooden refectory table, over which the couple presided—Hearst at one end and Davies at the other. Oddly, guests drew paper napkins from chrome dispensers and poured catsup from bottles placed along the tabletop.

Hearst's primary reason for throwing these gaudy weekend parties was to forward Davies' career. Hearst had discovered Davies in a Ziegfeld Follies chorus line and was obsessed with making her a star at any cost, no matter how long it took. To this end, he played producer to the films she was cast in, bankrolling the productions up to $1 million apiece. The plan nearly worked, as he landed her a long-term contract with Louis B.

Land O' Excess and Abuse

Mayer at MGM, where she had what must have been the most opulent dressing room ever—a two-story, fourteen-room Spanish-style villa, complete with works by Renoir on the walls.

But Davies' contract at MGM didn't last. When Mayer began letting better roles go to Irving Thalberg's wife, Norma Shearer, Hearst became irate and stormed into Mayer's office to demand that Davies be cast in the "surefire" Oscar-winning role of Marie Antoinette, which Thalberg had promised to his wife. Mayer decided Thalberg's genius was more important to him than Hearst's millions and told the tycoon to hit the bricks.

He did. Hearst called Jack Warner to tell him that he was bringing his business to Burbank. He then dispatched a construction crew to the MGM lot where, during the night, they dismantled Ms. Davies' dressing room—Renoirs and all—loaded it on several trucks, drove it over the Hollywood Hills, and set it up again at Warners. Jack Warner got more than a dressing room and a mediocre star that night; he got millions of dollars, the support of Hearst's many newspapers, and the powerful Louella Parsons, who owed her career to Hearst.

NOUVEAU HOLLYWOOD

Ever since the fifties, television has elbowed its way into the Hollywood scene; today television stars can switch to features, and film actors don't think twice before jumping into a cushy television gig. One could even argue that the moguls of today are television producers. Take Aaron Spelling, for example.

Spelling has made an indelible mark on television. He alone is responsible for *Charlie's Angels, Dynasty, Love Boat, Fantasy Island,* and over 150 other programs. It all adds up to an estimated personal worth over $250 million. Spelling set out to show it off, and he did in 1987, by building the Manor, the largest single-family dwelling in the state of California, at a cost of over $45 million.

The 65,000-square-foot (6,045-sq-m) structure, intended to house Spelling, his wife, Candy, and their two teenage children, has everything the average family of four needs: four bars, three kitchens, a theater, a gym, an Olympic-size swimming pool, a doll museum, a separate servants' wing, eight two-car garages, twelve fountains, six formal gardens, a bowling alley, and a wine cellar. Aside from the astronomical cost of building the Manor, the place has an operating budget of $75,000 a month. Harold Lloyd and Gloria Swanson are certainly spinning in their graves.

All through Hollywood's Golden Age, drug abuse remained hidden from view, that is, it was virtually nonexistent as far as the public was concerned. Abuse was hushed up immediately or explained away as "fatigue" when seen within the industry. One reason for this tolerance was that often the drugs were not illicit or recreational, but prescribed by physicians on studio payrolls. Perhaps the most famous victim of this Hollywood tragedy was Judy Garland.

When the young Judy Garland was cast as Dorothy in *The Wizard of Oz*, it was a mixed blessing. On the one hand, the role helped revive her faltering career and launched her into superstardom. On the other hand, it drove her to an addiction which ruined—and eventually took—her life.

MGM didn't want Judy Garland for the role of Dorothy; the studio felt the seventeen-year-old was too old for the part. When the producers finally convinced the studio to go with Garland, she was placed on a strict diet in order to keep her weight down to a more girlish size—and here the word "strict" is an understatement. Garland was commanded to fast every other day. On days when she was allowed to eat, she had chicken broth from the MGM commissary and nothing else. She was prescribed diet pills (amphetamines) to help her keep to the regimen. In this way, she was able to make it through the rigorous months of her singing-and-dancing starring role while eating virtually no solid food.

With her new stardom came a hectic lifestyle. She took to smoking four packs of cigarettes a day, gobbling uppers for meals and downers to get to sleep at night. By July 1947, a combination of overwork, a diet of pills, her tremendous insecurity, an abortion, the birth of a child (the child, Liza Minnelli, grew up to face difficulties of her own with alcohol and drugs but overcame them), and three marriages brought Garland, age twenty-five, to a nervous breakdown. At this point, Garland was sent to a sanitarium to recover and treat her addiction.

When she came out "cured," she was broke financially, and rushed back to work before she

They've great
respect for
the dead in
Hollywood, but
none for the
living.

— Errol Flynn

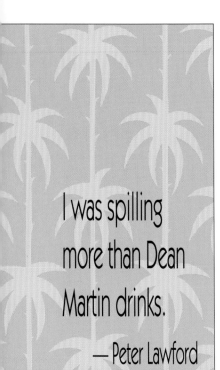

I was spilling more than Dean Martin drinks.

— Peter Lawford

was emotionally or physically ready. She soon collapsed again. She continued trying to work, showing up late—if at all—and unable to perform. Eventually MGM let her go. She made several suicide attempts. Following the death of her mother, she relied on more and more pills.

Her fourth husband, Sid Luft, gave her a new start when he produced the remake of *A Star Is Born* and cast her as the lead opposite James Mason. To get into shape for the role, Garland stepped up her pill intake. When shooting started, she appeared on the set thirty pounds (14 kg) lighter—but, according to cast and crew, she was extremely difficult to work with.

During the early fifties, as she busily worked to remain financially solvent, she discovered the drug Ritalin, which supposedly energized the user without the dangerous side effects of amphetamines. But the drug still ruled over her; she lived on Ritalin for the rest of her life, augmenting its effects with morphine and alcohol. Her performances suffered terribly.

In June 1969, Judy Garland went to bed, having taken her usual barbiturates to go to sleep. Sometime in the night she apparently awoke and took more. She died that night from what was ruled an accidental overdose. The pills that sustained her career and her life, in the end, took them both away.

Many stars struggled with addiction, suffering silently while they grappled with the demands Hollywood made of them. It wasn't until the late forties, when the facade of Hollywood itself began to show wear and tear, that drugs again became an open symbol of Hollywood excess. One of the first stars whose drug use was exposed was Robert Mitchum.

In 1948, the public was still in the dark about Hollywood drug use, and the movie colony itself denied there was a problem. But Los Angeles Police Detective Sergeant Alva Barr knew what was going on and spearheaded a major crackdown on drug use in movieland. Tipped off about Mitchum by an informer, Barr and his assistants followed the actor for weeks, eventually gaining information that led them to the Hollywood cottage of his friend Lila Leeds. While standing outside the cottage, the police watched as Mitchum and a friend arrived and passed around some marijuana. As the group lit up, the police rushed in and made their arrests. Shortly after, Barr announced his plans for a major drug

Below: James Mason and Judy Garland in **A Star Is Born**, *1954.*

Booze is liquid suicide. I know booze can throw me down and kill me. Grass is better for you. I use a lot of it.

—Sterling Hayden

cleanup in Hollywood; the press reacted quite indignantly, reminding those in the community that the Wallace Reid scandal and "The Doom Book" had nearly destroyed the film industry two decades before.

Mitchum plea-bargained for a charge of "conspiracy to possess" marijuana (thereby waiving a trial and the need to testify). He was sentenced to sixty days in the county jail and two years' probation; he spent most of the sixty-day jail sentence in a minimum-security work camp where he received a constant stream of visitors, including Howard Hughes.

Mitchum was convinced the arrest would ruin his career. He stated his occupation as "former actor" and told reporters at the police station, "I'm ruined. I'm all washed up in pictures now I guess." That was not the case; the actor survived the debacle and signed a contract with Hughes to film *Holiday Affair* with Janet Leigh. In fact, Mitchum became more popular than ever.

Ironically, Mitchum, the target of the police "spearhead," was hardly a crazed drug addict but simply a casual user. In his probation report, he described his association with drugs, remarking on how he had been working very hard over the past two years and smoked marijuana only in the company of others who smoked, claiming that it relaxed him. His connection to the drug hardly seemed severe, even for that time.

Errol Flynn was frank about his drug use during this era, citing his experiences with marijuana, opium, and morphine in his colorful autobiography, *My Wicked, Wicked Ways*. In it, he described smoking marijuana with Mexican painter Diego Rivera, who took Flynn to his studio to *hear* his paintings. Sure enough, Flynn "heard these pictures singing: the simple Mexican themes . . . illumination and colour and sound in a symphony I could see, feel and hear—but can never translate into words."

Flynn's lusty quest for experience led him to try opium. He wrote: "My life came before me. It made sense . . . there was this beauty inside me, looking into my eyes with what I believed was true tenderness, even passion." In the same passage he later discounts the notion that opiates reduce sexual desire in males. "Dr. Flynn can tell you that such is not the case," he wrote, "I made love to Ting Ling in ways . . . I would never believe myself capable of."

Bela Lugosi, the star of *Dracula* and the subject of the next big Hollywood drug scandal, sent the message to the public about the potential dangers of taking drugs. In 1955 Lugosi entered Los Angeles General Hospital seeking a cure for his secret methadone addiction—an addiction he claimed to have suffered with for twenty years.

His use of the drug began to taper off around 1953, but poor health and his failing career lead him to resume heavy use; by the time he had checked himself into the hospital, the actor could hardly find a place on his legs for the injections. He discussed his withdrawal with reporters:

> I cannot describe the tortures I underwent. My body grew hot, then cold. I tried to eat the bed sheets, my pajamas. My heart beat madly— then it seemed to stop . . . I used to take five or six needles a day. And when I took the cure they took it all away from me . . . . It was horrible, horrible.

Lugosi was released three months later and resumed making B movies. He described being cured as "the greatest thing that ever happened

to me," but his happiness was short-lived; he died within a year—and was buried in Count Dracula's black cape.

Times certainly were changing as the sixties came rushing in. The studio system gasped its last few breaths; rock music and television were stealing audiences away from the movies; and Cary Grant, the elegant leading man from Hollywood's Golden Age, was experimenting with LSD.

Grant was fifty-five years old in 1959, battling with the constant mental stress that came with his stardom. He had begun seeing Dr. Mortimer Hartman, a prominent Beverly Hills psychotherapist, to try to ease his anguish. Hartman decided to include Grant in an experimental program he was conducting and began injecting him with weekly doses of LSD to aid in his therapy. After the injections, Grant would lay on the doctor's

ONLY IN HOLLYWOOD . . .

Gloria Swanson was known as "the second woman in Hollywood to earn $1 million (after Mary Pickford) and the first to spend it." She was renowned for never wearing any dress more than twice.

Rudy Vallee tried to have the name of his street in Beverly Hills changed to Rue de Vallee. Neighbors banded together to put down his proposal. Vallee called them all "a bunch of disgruntled pukes." Cecil B. De Mille had more clout in town; he lived on De Mille Drive.

Clara Bow had her limousine painted a flaming red to match her hair color. She always traveled with two pet Chows, which she also had dyed to match the ensemble.

Silent screen star Francis X. Bushman kept three hundred Great Danes on his opulent California estate.

When Ginger Rogers arrived in London to play *Mame* on stage, she disembarked with 118 pieces of luggage.

Howard Hughes spent $12 million trying to buy up every print of his box office flop *The Conqueror*. The film cost $6 million to produce.

Rin Tin Tin was the only dog in America with a personal chef, a valet, his own limousine and chauffeur, and a five-room dressing complex on the studio lot.

Steven Spielberg wanted to thank the four leading cast members in his film *Always*. On the last day of shooting, John Goodman, Richard Dreyfuss, Holly Hunter, and Brad Johnson arrived to find brand-new red Mazda Miatas with personalized plates in their parking spots.

couch and relive his worst nightmares while Hartman talked him through it all. Grant cried, feeling he could see himself for what he really was, truthfully, for the first time in his life. He was sold on LSD and gave himself over to the treatments. He convinced his wife at the time, Betsy Drake—and even his household help—to take the therapy, going as far as to pay for some of their sessions.

Cary Grant was elated by the drug and vowed to tell the world about what LSD had done for him. Shortly after his revelation, he began work on *Operation Petticoat* for Universal. While on location, he gave an informal interview to columnist Joe Hyams, telling him he'd been "born again" and that he'd "been through a psychiatric experience" that had changed his life. "It was horrendous," he told Hyams. "I had to face

things about myself which I never admitted, which I didn't know were there . . . . I was an utter fake, a self-opinionated bore, a know-all who knew very little."

Grant eventually allowed Hyams to publish the interview, but the night before the series of articles was to appear, he had a change of heart. He called Hyams and demanded the interview be pulled. But it was too late. The next day the world knew that a big star had used LSD and was in psychotherapy. And yet, the revelation did little to harm Grant's image; *Operation Petticoat*, which opened shortly afterward, was a hit.

Grant continued to use LSD frequently until the substance was banned from therapeutic use in 1963. His use of LSD may have been a factor in his marital problems with Drake—after several sessions with the drug, she refused to continue

Right: Cary Grant and Tony Curtis face off in **Operation Petticoat,** *Grant's first film after his LSD enlightenment.*

Left: Reformed Hollywood bad boy Dennis Hopper with his wife, Kathleen, in 1990.

the controversial treatments. Others close to Grant at the time claim the drug affected his memory and ability to work, but he always denied it and—no one knows for sure.

The mild public reaction to Grant's experimentation with LSD, as early as 1959, foretold a somewhat relaxed attitude toward drug use in America, and especially in Hollywood during the sixties, an attitude that was well expressed in Dennis Hopper's megahit *Easy Rider* in 1969. The film, about a pair of bikers transporting a stash of cocaine, won Hopper a well-deserved second chance in Hollywood. He had become an industry pariah in the late fifties by being extremely difficult to work with. For example, he tried forcing Method acting on John Wayne, his reluctant costar in *From Hell to Texas*—it didn't work on the Duke.

Hopper's second chance came and went in a hurry. His next project after *Easy Rider* was a multimillion dollar fiasco shot in South America called *The Last Movie* (it very nearly was for Hopper),

which was pulled by American distributors less than two weeks after its release. Hopper was a Hollywood outcast again and he disappeared for the remainder of the seventies and half of the next decade, retreating to a house in Taos, New Mexico, where he and a group of friends drowned themselves under, as he put it, "mountains of cocaine and gallons of booze." They lived lives of real-life western outlaws, even engaging in gun battles with locals who were bent on purging the area of Hopper and his long-haired friends. He struggled through a troubled eight-day marriage to Michelle Phillips, ex-singer of the Mamas and the Papas, and all the while he kept up the drug and alcohol abuse—drinking half a gallon (2 l) of rum, a few beers and doing three grams of cocaine a day—thinking it was okay to self-destruct because he was an artist.

In 1983 he reached absolute bottom while on location in Mexico. One night Hopper went to his tent drunk and awoke thinking he heard people being tortured and killed outside. He

A LITTLE EXTRA INSURANCE

Stars often credit their success to more than just charisma. It is easy to tell what they find important: Just look at their insurance policies.

Rudolph Valentino, Douglas Fairbanks, and Mary Pickford all had "scarred-face policies," just in case their most valuable asset was ever damaged. Pickford's policy was worth $1 million.

Cross-eyed Ben Turpin took out a policy for $100,000 against the remote possibility of his eyes ever *righting* themselves.

Leading man Edmund Lowe insured his handsome nose for $35,000. And Jimmy Durante knew what side his bread was buttered on; he insured his famous schnozz for $100,000.

Anthony Quinn once shaved his head for his role in *The Magus*. He was insured heavily in the event that his hair did not grow back.

Betty Grable, the "girl with the million-dollar legs," actually had her gams insured for $1,250,000. Cyd Charisse's long, lovely legs were insured for $10 million. And smooth Fred Astaire covered his for a cool million.

panicked and ran off in order to escape. The next morning he was found naked and incoherent, stumbling along a Mexico highway. He checked into a treatment center in Los Angeles and went straight shortly after.

Today, a clean and sober Dennis Hopper is back on top of the Hollywood hierarchy, starring in hit films like *Blue Velvet* and *River's Edge* as well as directing features. He married a fourth time—to a ballerina about thirty years his junior. Looking back, Hopper once remarked, "I was lucky to get out of the seventies alive." Perhaps the same could be said for Hollywood in general.

One of the men who saved Hollywood from the doldrums of the seventies was Steven Spielberg, who, along with a handful of other filmmakers in the late seventies, made movies with lots of action and fantasy that appealed to younger audiences, giving a fading industry a much-needed shot in the arm. Coming into the eighties, the industry was stronger than ever. Hollywood was again awash in megadollars.

But with all its wealth, Hollywood went drug-crazy. At the 1981 Academy Awards Johnny Carson quipped "the biggest money-maker in Hollywood last year was Colombia. [Pause.] Not the studio—the country." Certainly, drug use among the rich and famous had reached a saturation point. In fact, the problem was so pervasive that insurance companies began amending studio production insurance policies to reflect drug-related risks. That same year, police cracked a cocaine ring that catered to the stars in the Hollywood Hills by delivering the goods in a chauffeured limousine.

National attention was once again drawn to Hollywood; a House Select Committee on Narcotics Abuse and Control came to town to hold a series of hearings to investigate drug use in the Hollywood community. But few stars volunteered to testify before the Committee after cries of witch-hunting were heard, evoking the dark anticommunist days of the fifties. The Committee left town knowing little more than it did when it arrived. It seemed the community was intent on keeping its drug problem intact and well hidden.

A little more than a year later, the death of comedian-actor John Belushi in a bungalow at the famed Chateau Marmont hotel on Sunset Boulevard changed all that. His life of outrageous excess and his death by lethal injection of cocaine and heroin seemed to be just too much. (For details, see page 144.) Suddenly, Hollywood knew it had a problem. As the decade wore on, more and more cases of stars with drug and alcohol problems surfaced as careers were interrupted for treatment—Ali MacGraw, Liza Minnelli, Ally Sheedy, and Robin Williams are just a few examples. Slowly, the general attitude toward drugs and alcohol began to become much more conservative.

Above: Wildman John Belushi in his 1941 garb.

Clean and sober. Above: Actress-writer Carrie Fisher. Opposite: Richard Dreyfuss in 1991.

herself rummaging through medicine cabinets at New York parties, looking for prescription drugs to steal.

In 1985, after a painful low and a moment of self-revelation, she checked herself into a rehabilitation center. While recovering, she was approached by *Esquire* magazine to write some nonfiction pieces on Hollywood which eventually became her semiautobiographical novel *Postcards From the Edge*. (She also wrote the screenplay for the hit film). Her writing career took off from there, helping to pull her safely away from drugs. She now considers herself a former addict with a vengeance or, as she puts it, "Joan of Narc, or patron saint of the addict."

Richard Dreyfuss is an even more extreme example of an actor who nearly lost everything to his drug abuse, but somehow managed a very successful rebound.

Dreyfuss's drug problem began as far back as 1966, when, as a conscientious objector during the Vietnam war, he performed alternative service in a Los Angeles hospital. It was there that he developed a habit for readily available amphetamines. He was able to kick that habit but later picked up a lethal combination of cognac and cocaine.

Dreyfuss reached the pinnacle of stardom by the age of thirty-three, winning an Oscar for his performance in *The Goodbye Girl* and making box-office history in *Close Encounters of the Third Kind*. Meanwhile, he was doing a lot of drugs, often drinking and snorting entire nights away with his friend Carrie Fisher. He followed his huge successes with a string of flops—choices he now chalks up to drug-impaired judgment. It was during his career low that he, too, discovered Percodan. He took to making a movie every eighteen months in order to leave, as he told *Newsweek* in 1987, "lots of time for drugs."

Dreyfuss hit bottom in October 1982, when he drove his Mercedes convertible into a palm tree; he flipped the car over and was trapped inside for two hours. He was hospitalized and arrested for possession of cocaine. To recover fully, Dreyfuss took a break from filmmaking for

Carrie Fisher is one star who conquered her drug problem. She spent her childhood in the public eye as the daughter of Debbie Reynolds and Eddie Fisher. The stardom she achieved with her role as Princess Leia in *Star Wars* allowed her finally to make the move away from her mother; she went to New York where she fell in with the crowd at *Saturday Night Live*, whose ringleader happened to be John Belushi. In 1983 she married her long-time friend, singer Paul Simon, but the troubled marriage lasted only eleven months. To dampen the pain and heartache of the divorce, she relied heavily on the drugs she'd begun to take—Percodan and LSD. "Drugs," she told *Time* magazine, "became a way of blunting the sharpness of the juts." She became more and more dependent on the drugs until she found

It wasn't the drugs that bothered me. It was the way people acted on 'em. They behaved like blithering idiots, acid casualties.

—Steve Martin

I don't do the Hollywood party scene anymore. You can't come home and say to the kid, "Hi, here's a little switch. Daddy's going to throw up on you."

— Robin Williams

Above: Drew Barrymore, child star of E.T. *Opposite: Paul Newman suits up for his true passion, auto racing.*

three years in order to get his life and family back together. His second chance arrived in 1985, when Paul Mazursky gave him the lead role in his movie *Down and Out in Beverly Hills*. The movie was a real hit, and Dreyfuss was back on top, making a startling comeback after being on the brink of disaster. Dreyfuss told *Newsweek* after his recovery, "I find that working is better than snorting."

Stories of decadence and recovery were common in Hollywood during the eighties. The tragedies averted by adults like Fisher and Dreyfuss came even closer to consuming the young life of Drew Barrymore—last in a long line of thespian Barrymores famous for acting and alcoholism.

The tiny, talented six-year-old Barrymore was thrust into the spotlight of worldwide fame following her role in the tremendous hit *E.T.* Almost immediately afterward, she felt the stress of a life in the upper strata of Hollywood. By the time she

was nine years old, she was being invited to nightclubs and parties and trying to cope with all the attention while struggling with problems at home. Barrymore took her first drink at the age of nine; she was smoking marijuana by the age of ten; she was snorting cocaine when she was twelve. Her fourteenth year brought her to the brink of suicide.

At that time, she was stumbling along, drinking, taking drugs, and bouncing in and out of a rehabilitation center. Finally, depressed, broke, and home alone, she cut her wrist with a kitchen knife. The opportune arrival of her roommate saved her; today she is clean and sober, but admits it is a struggle to remain so.

As stories like these began to make headlines, they brought about a change in Hollywood's view of drugs. Slowly, almost imperceptibly, attitudes shifted, drug users and abusers fell out of vogue, and the blatant public consumption of cocaine once again disappeared

BETWEEN TAKES: HOLLYWOOD HOBBIES AND PASTIMES

Robert Conrad
Flying

Billy Crystal
Baseball

Jamie Lee Curtis
Skiing

Tony Curtis
Assemblages, painting

Kirk Douglas
Writing novels, collecting pre-Colombian art

Robert Downey, Jr.
Writing poetry

Blake Edwards
Painting, sculpting

Michael J. Fox
Reading history

Dennis Hopper
Photography

Diane Keaton
Photography

Jay Leno
Auto racing

underground. Today, fewer stars are addicts, and those who are rarely admit to their dependency. Stars now seem to spend their money on more socially acceptable diversions—working out with personal trainers, health food, and bars that serve only imported bottle water are now common-place—and seek their thrills in a less self-destructive manner.

Some celebrities prefer to take their chances riding vintage Harley-Davidsons in celebrity biker gangs. Sylvester Stallone, Mickey Rourke, Priscilla Presley, and even Gary Busey (despite a near-fatal motorcycle accident) all patronize Bartel's, a Culver City Harley-Davidson shop that caters to stars. More recently, rock and roll singer-actor Billy Idol crashed while riding and narrowly escaped death. He now performs his energetic act with a limp and a cane—and continues to ride. Still, the dangerous, exciting hobby con-tinues to grow in popularity with the Hollywood elite. Concerned producers have even begun putting "no ride" riders on star contracts, attempting to secure their investments.

To some stars, the freedom and speed a motorcycle offers just isn't enough; to them, pro-fessional auto racing is the ultimate thrill. Most notable for racing cars are Steve McQueen and Paul Newman, who discovered the sport while filming the movie *Winning* in 1969. And it was Newman who turned his costar in *The Color of Money*, Tom Cruise, on to racing, giving him a spot on his team and the inspiration to develop his own racing movie, *Days of Thunder*.

Gene Hackman also races cars semiprofes-sionally and flies planes as well—another chic celebrity thrill. Hackman flies an open-pit biplane; as he puts it, the "rush of the wind in the face is unbeatable." Cliff Robertson, Christopher Reeve, and John Travolta are also among Hollywood's high-flyers.

The latest hobby stars have taken up in their quest to find the greatest thrill—without abusing their bodies—is marksmanship. They offer dif-ferent reasons for learning to shoot handguns, from preparation for a particular role to working out their frustrations on targets. But almost all of

these celebrities frequent the posh and exclusive Beverly Hills Gun Club, which has been host to such star marksmen as Emilio Estevez, Charlie Sheen, Billy Crystal, Jamie Lee Curtis, Sean Penn, Sylvester Stallone, and Arnold Schwarzenegger, who is a partner at the Club.

Of course, when stars take up recreational activities, they often get a different experience than the rest of us. In 1989 a group of Hollywood's most powerful, including Tom Cruise, Tom Selleck, Disney Studio chief Jeffrey Katzenberg, and producer Don Simpson, went "roughing it" on a river rafting trip in Wyoming. Following close behind them was a second raft carrying a group of people whose job was "to make sure they [the stars] were all safe." Also aboard the second raft was a private chef and an entire catering staff. Roughing it, indeed.

I just drank a lot—out of boredom, pressure, frustration. Then a couple of years ago I thought, "What on earth am I doing, drinking myself into oblivion?" So I quit it ... There's more to life than getting soused every night.

— Rock Hudson

CHAPTER SEVEN

Feudin' Hollywood

In some ways, Hollywood is like a small town—everybody knows everybody. When gigantic egos start tromping around in such a confined area, toes are bound to get stepped on and tempers are bound to flare. It's been that way since the studios' earliest days, when mega lomaniacal bosses tried to keep eccentric creative types in tow.

In the early days, feuds with studio bosses were always rare—not because they were such nice guys but because the power they held was too great and they could easily reduce employees to groveling. Harry Cohn, the studio chief of Columbia Pictures, was infamously vindictive and never bothered with subtleties. Once, a maverick writer dared to argue with Cohn over script changes the mogul had ordered. The two

bellowed away at the top of their lungs until Cohn seemed to back down, telling the writer to go home for the weekend and think over his suggestions. As the writer left the lot, Cohn hailed a group of studio carpenters and plasterers and ordered them to go to the building where the writer worked. When the writer returned to the studio on Monday morning to report to his office, he couldn't find it. His door had been walled up and plastered over.

Writers have traditionally been low on the Hollywood totem pole, but stars have always had a little more power and have occasionally used it to get back at studio bosses. The Marx Brothers, for instance, had a real flair for comebacks.

MGM producer Irving Thalberg, who produced two of the Marx Brothers' biggest hits, *A*

Opposite: Jack Nicholson gets the point in Chinatown. *Below: Groucho and Harpo Marx get even in* A Night at the Opera.

Night at the Opera and *A Day at the Races*, had an annoying habit of making visitors wait for hours before they were allowed to see him. The Marx Brothers were no exception. One day, after waiting nearly two hours for a meeting with Thalberg, the comedians decided they'd had enough.

First, they tied Thalberg's secretary to her chair. They broke the outer office furniture into kindling and used It to start a fire just outside Thalberg's door, fanning the smoke underneath it and into his office. When they heard the producer stir inside, they pushed filing cabinets against the door. Thalberg was forced to escape out the window. He ran around the building and burst into his reception area; there were the Marx Brothers, sitting around the fire in their underwear, toasting marshmallows and feeding them to the secretary, still tied to the chair.

Thalberg never kept them waiting again.

In the forties, Hollywood was full of people who settled their differences in a more direct manner, like director John Huston and swash-buckler Errol Flynn.

In his book *City of Nets*, Otto Friedrich recounts a scene at a party at David O. Selznick's home, in which Huston overheard Flynn make an off-color remark—"something wretched"— about Olivia de Havilland. Huston snapped at Flynn, "That's a lie! Even if it weren't a lie, only a son of a bitch would repeat it!" Flynn asked Huston if he wanted to make something of it; Huston said he did. They excused themselves from the party and went outside.

Out in the garden, the two men removed their jackets and began a fight that lasted for the better part of an hour. They battled away, undetected, until headlights from

What are you, the Pope or something?

— Harry Cohn, to rebellious director Frank Capra

Above: There was no love lost between Ray Milland and Marlene Dietrich on the set of Golden Earrings, *1947.*

into her mouth, sucked an eyeball out of it, and then stuck a finger down her throat and retched. The performance was a success—Milland became "violently ill."

Tough-as-nails Kate Hepburn could also feud with the best of them. While working on *Suddenly, Last Summer*, Hepburn deplored the treatment of costar Montgomery Clift by the director, Joseph Mankiewicz, who considered Clift a self-indulgent brat and constantly browbeat the actor. Hepburn took to Clift and nursed him through his drug and alcohol problems; it was only with her help that he managed to even finish the picture. When the last scene was shot and the crew was wrapping up, Hepburn asked Mankiewicz if he was quite sure neither she nor Clift would be called for retakes or other business with him. When the director assured her that was correct, Hepburn ceremoniously spit in his face.

Bette Davis was a Hollywood star with huge talent and an ego to match. Consequently, she was a virtual lightning rod for bitter interpersonal conflicts; her feud with Joan Crawford is par for the Davis course.

The two stars were often in competition for the same roles throughout their careers and were prone to holding a grudge—especially Crawford, whose jealousy of Jean Harlow, according to Crawford's biographer Bob Thomas, bitterly divided the MGM lot in the thirties. A friend of Crawford's, co-MGM starlet Dorothy Manners attended the wedding of Harlow and cameraman Harold Rosson. When Dorothy later saw Joan, she was called on the carpet. "What were you doing there," Joan demanded. "I was invited," replied Manners. "Well, you can't be her friend and mine, too," said Crawford. When Manners asked why not, Crawford simply said, "Because you can't." Manners eventually abandoned her friendship with Harlow.

It's easy to see how animosity might grow between Crawford and Davis. But their feud, as such, didn't materialize until they had each reached the age of fifty-four and settled into semiretirement. At the time, Crawford was managing her late husband's business affairs with the

the cars of guests leaving the party illuminated them. Selznick was able to break up the fight, and the men were sent to the hospital— Flynn for two broken ribs, Huston for a broken nose. Years later, Huston remembered that Flynn had called him to ask about his condition. At the time he told Flynn that he had "thoroughly enjoyed the fight" and sincerely hoped they could "do it again some time."

Marlene Dietrich had her own special way of getting back at an adversary. She had decided to end three years of semiretirement to play a seductive Gypsy in *Golden Earrings*. Upon returning to Hollywood, she caught wind of rumors that her costar in the picture, Ray Milland, was unhappy about playing love scenes with "an old bag" and had, in fact, threatened to walk out of the project on account of her.

Tensions on the set were strained and would occasionally flare up as the two made love on-camera and waged war off it. It was Dietrich, though, who got the last laugh; near the end of the shooting came the scene where Milland meets the Gypsy Dietrich as she stirs a large pot of stew. As cameras rolled and Milland approached, she pulled a fish head out of the stew, popped it

Right: Bette Davis and Joan Crawford in **Whatever Happened to Baby Jane?,** *1962.*

for failing to see the charm in Flynn's hiding a live snake in her panties.

Joan Fontaine muttered curses under her breath at Cary Grant during the filming of *Suspicion* and she even publicly called him "an incredible bore."

George Raft and Edward G. Robinson clashed on- and off-screen over the affections of costar Marlene Dietrich—who found more to like in tough-guy Raft—on the set of *Manpower*.

Dirk Bogarde looked forward to working with his idol, Judy Garland, in *I Could Go on Singing*. When they first began working together, he addressed her as "Miss Garland"; by the end of the project, he was referring to her as "It."

Pepsi-Cola company and Davis had returned to the stage. Joan was looking for a project that the two mature actresses might act in together and found it in a novel called *Whatever Happened to Baby Jane?* Bette agreed the project was perfect and they went ahead looking for a studio to produce it. It was a difficult task, as none of the major studios wanted to risk making a film whose stars were over fifty years old. Crawford found an independent production company to pick up the tab and that whet the interest of Jack Warner, another of Bette's old nemeses, who agreed to distribute the film.

As the picture went into production, the stars denied rumors of a feud and, seeing the project as an important and much-needed boost to their careers, promised to be cooperative. A publicist for the film alerted *Time* magazine, and a story about the production appeared in the publication. The next day on the set Davis asked the publicist if she was responsible for the article. When she answered that she was, Davis snapped, "She [Crawford] is five years older than me if she's a day." Crawford, on the other hand, was pleased with the piece and told the publicist, "We're off to a good start, aren't we?"

Davis quickly became pals with director Bob Aldrich. But Crawford considered Aldrich "her director" and resented Davis for acting as if the

project were her idea. Tensions on the set mounted but, somehow, the film was shot on schedule and with few flare-ups between the two stars.

It was during the publicity tour that the famous feud came alive.

The two actresses were scheduled to tour 150 cinemas—seventy-five each. Crawford backed out of her commitment and, much to her consternation, Davis agreed to tour all 150 theaters! While on tour, during an interview on television, Davis told how hard it was getting a studio to back a movie with "two old broads" as stars; she promptly got an extremely angry letter from Crawford instructing her never to refer to her as such.

The film was a big hit and brought Davis an Oscar nomination (often a source of antagonism in Hollywood). Crawford, who was not nominated, felt slighted by the Academy and began to openly campaign against Davis. She even offered to accept the award for Anne Bancroft, another nominee that year, should she be unable to attend the awards ceremony—just so she could upstage Davis.

The night of the Oscars, Crawford swept into the Santa Monica Civic Auditorium early, grabbing the largest dressing room and installing huge Pepsi coolers backstage stocked with liquor. The

All actors get preoccupied with billing order, but I've learned it doesn't matter a damn as long as your name's in the same size type.

— Charlton Heston

Sin City

tension between Davis and Crawford was palpable, and when Bancroft was announced as the winner of the Best Actress Oscar—for her performance in *The Miracle Worker*—Crawford pushed Davis aside with a triumphant "Ha!" and walked proudly on stage to thunderous applause to accept for Bancroft.

Baby Jane was such a success that the two actresses were set to star in *Hush . . . Hush, Sweet Charlotte*; but there was even more tension between them after the Oscar trauma. Davis had taken to referring to Crawford as "Bless-you," as in "I hope Bless-you doesn't insist on working in subzero temperatures when we get back to the studio." The extreme tension and pressure on the set probably helped bring on the "upper respiratory" illness in Crawford, who was admitted to a hospital soon after the start of the project. She was replaced by Olivia de Havilland, who happened to be a good friend of Davis. Crawford was irate and vowed that while she would make more pictures in the future, she planned to "make them with decent, gentle people."

Davis continued to cause friction through her entire career, even on the set of *The Whales of August*, a film in which the median age of the actors matched that of Davis—eighty. Davis appeared opposite Lillian Gish, who was in her nineties at the time, and she was irked that Gish had a meatier role. After one particularly good performance in close-up, everyone congratulated Gish—except Davis who cracked, "She should be good at close-ups . . . the bitch *invented* them." Gish took advantage of her years and played up her hearing loss, pretending not to hear a word—but only when Davis was speaking.

Just as Oscar fever brought the Davis and Crawford feud to a boil, the same obsessive object of desire—the gold-plated Oscar statuette—caused a divisive rift between sisters Olivia de Havilland and Joan Fontaine.

De Havilland was crushed when she lost the Best Supporting Actress Oscar to Hattie McDaniel, also for *Gone With The Wind*, in 1940. Her disappointment grew not simply because she didn't get the award; Jack Warner saw her loss as an

opportunity to relegate her to a string of lesser roles opposite Errol Flynn. The nomination had sparked an appetite for an Oscar and de Havilland deeply regretted the more minor roles that followed her loss. She was lucky enough to be nominated two years later for her role in *Hold Back the Dawn*, but lost that year to her sister Joan, who won for her role in *Suspicion*.

The loss enraged Olivia (she was the one who dared her sister to try and be an actress in the first place). Driven by Oscar fever, de Havilland left Jack Warner and MGM, successfully suing the studio to achieve her independence in a historic legal milestone, now called "The de Havilland Decision." It was a long, hard struggle, but by 1946 she was back from the brink and had garnered a nomination for *To Each His Own*. The sisters—both in attendance at the awards that year—were seated separately by nervous Academy planners, never eager for a scene at the ceremony. That year, de Havilland finally got her wish, winning the Oscar for Best Actress. On her way back to her table, according to Peter H. Brown in his book *Oscar Dearest*, Joan reached out to congratulate her. De Havilland thrust up her chin and pushed quickly by. "Do you know what she said as I tried to congratulate her?" said Fontaine later. "Do you know what my own sister said? She said, 'Ugh!'"

During Hollywood's Golden Age, every little bit of interpersonal bickering and every cold-blooded, lifelong feud was aired in public by those two giants of Hollywood gossip, Hedda Hopper and Louella Parsons. Ironically, the feud that raged between the columnists themselves often overshadowed—and has outlived—much of the gossip they spread around in their heyday, during which the two women achieved a staggering daily readership of fifty million.

Hedda Hopper started her show business career in New York City as an actress and the fifth

HOLLYWOOD PUT-DOWNS

There, but for the grace of God, goes God.
—Herman J. Mankiewicz, on Orson Welles

Joan Crawford? I wouldn't sit on her toilet!
—Bette Davis

Working with [Julie Andrews] is like being hit over the head with a Valentine card.
—Christopher Plummer

Bogey's a helluva nice guy until 11:30 P.M. After that he thinks he's Bogart.
—Dave Chasen

Most of the time [Marlon Brando] sounds like he has a mouthful of wet toilet paper.
—Rex Reed

[Gary Cooper]'s got a reputation as a great actor just by thinking hard about the next line.
—King Vidor

I can't imagine any guy giving [Bette Davis] a tumble.
—Carl Laemmle

[Errol Flynn was] a fifty-year trespass against good taste.
—Leslie Mallory

To tell the truth, [Clark Gable] isn't such a helluva good lay.
—Carole Lombard

Mother was the real-life Wicked Witch of the West.
—Liza Minnelli, on Judy Garland

[Marilyn Monroe is] . . . a professional amateur.
—Laurence Olivier

wife of DeWolf Hopper, a legendary stage actor and ladies' man. Upon her divorce from Hopper she made her way to Hollywood, where her career was more "off-again" than "on-again." It was during one of these slow periods, in 1936, that a friend suggested Hedda apply her great interest in shopping and clothes to another pursuit and write a Hollywood fashion column. She was already in her fifties when Hedda Hopper became Hollywood's newest gossip.

The established Louella Parsons, the grand dame of Tinseltown gossip (who had treated Hedda fairly, if infrequently, in her column) barely gave the arrival of her new rival any notice at all;

in fact, when a party was thrown to welcome Hopper into the fold of Hollywood journalists, Louella was conspicuously absent. Some say the feud between the two began that day.

George Gells, in his book *Hedda and Louella*, says Hopper wasted no time baring her claws. After a particularly vicious piece about Merle Oberon appeared in her column, the actress asked Hedda why she'd written it. Her response was, "Bitchery, dear. Sheer bitchery." Even the great Louella Parsons was not off-limits to Hopper's barbs, prompting Louella to snap, "She's trying to do in two years what took me thirty and I resent some of the things she says about me." Soon the two women were trading barbs in print.

When Bette Davis gave birth to her first baby, she quietly disappeared from the public eye, refusing all interviews. Hopper suspected Davis was hiding out in her Laguna Beach cottage. She drove down to the cottage, found the door open, and walked in to get the scoop. Louella later remarked in her column that "Since Bette Davis has had so many unwelcome visitors, she has had to have her gate padlocked." Around town, there was no doubt who the "unwanted visitor" was.

The two columnists carried on like this for a decade; then, in 1948, an official cease-fire was called; the two women met for lunch at Romanoff's in Beverly Hills, apparently to bury the hatchet. They carried on in an extremely polite manner for all the public to see—the feud had apparently run its course. Hopper told Louella at the meeting, "Darling, if you and I ever get together and compare notes, we'll rock this town on its heels."

It's not surprising the feud ended as it did; Hopper was never one to carry a grudge. She once kept an energetic feud going with Marlene Dietrich for a full year but finally had to call Dietrich's business manager to ask exactly what it was she had been angry at Dietrich about in the first place.

Hedda and Louella were able to patch things up. But another great duo from the forties was not quite so fortunate. After a bitter split that ended a ten-year relationship as a highly successful comedy team, Dean Martin and Jerry Lewis still aren't talking.

Martin and Lewis had been a smash hit since they met in 1946. Their act, with Martin as the singing straight man and Lewis as the clown, carried them with equal success from nightclubs right into movies. After working together on a long string of comedies, they began to drift apart. Lewis was interested in writing and directing their pictures; according to Lewis' autobiography, *Jerry Lewis, In Person*, Martin was interested in anything but their work and was usually off playing golf. Other sources have painted a picture of Lewis as a megalomaniac on the set, a perfectionist who had to have everything his way. As Lewis tells it,

Below: Hopper's competition, the grand dame of the gossip game, Louella Parsons.

Above: Jerry Lewis is "still waiting" for Dean Martin (right) to kiss and make up.

with hope, ready to patch up the twenty-year rift. He sent a letter to Martin's hotel, but received no response. Weeks passed and Lewis sent another letter. Again, Martin did not respond. Months later, Lewis was in Las Vegas where Martin was performing and left a message for him. Martin, responding through a third party, said he would meet Lewis at the Sahara Hotel at four P.M.

As Lewis put it in his autobiography, "I'm still waiting."

More recently, Hollywood movie stars have learned to "play nice," limiting their infighting and outbursts to a cutdown mumbled here, a witty line dropped there. However, Cher once described Peter Bogdanovich, her director in *Mask*, as a "pig." Debra Winger revealed in a television interview that the emotion she displayed in love scenes with Richard Gere in *An Officer and a Gentleman* was not lust but disgust. News from the set during the filming of *Outrageous Fortune* was sketchy, but with two giant stars with egos to match, Bette Midler and Shelley Long, sparks had to fly. But the only proof we have is in the resulting advertising campaign in which Long was billed first on one side of the country and Midler billed first on the other.

It seems surprising that two actors as different in temperament as Marlon Brando and Burt Reynolds should even know each other, let alone despise one another, but there is little love lost between them. Apparently their physical similarity is the root of it all.

he made an appeal to Martin, hoping to spark feelings for what they once had together. Martin's response, according to Lewis, was, "You can talk about love all you want. To me, you're nothing but a dollar sign." That was the beginning of the end. It was in 1956, not long after that comment, that Lewis quit his contract with Martin—a nearly devastating move financially.

Lewis continued to work hard, writing and directing one of his most popular films, *The Nutty Professor*, just a few years later. Some critics consider the film a blatant parody of Dean Martin as a selfish, slippery ladies' man.

The two did not speak again for many years, until the "Jerry Lewis Telethon" in 1976. During the broadcast, Frank Sinatra came out and announced that he had "a friend" backstage he wanted Jerry to meet. Out walked Dean Martin; Lewis and Martin embraced, and after the show Lewis was filled

Above: James Woods got a little too close to Sean Young while costarring in The Boost, *1988.*

The Boost—Hollywood "bad boy" James Woods and Hollywood oddball-actress Sean Young, whose reputation for being extremely hard to work with has made her somewhat of a black sheep in Tinseltown.

While shooting the steamy love scenes in *The Boost*, the two actors began an affair that became common knowledge to everyone on the set. Woods' fiancée at the time, Sarah Owen, was understandably upset and demanded that the two break it off. Young resisted, even showing up at Woods' house one night after work (Owen kicked her out, then kicked Woods in the groin); eventually the relationship seemed to be over.

But the trouble was just beginning.

Young's reputation for difficult behavior again came to life on the set of *The Boost*. Young, who carried around a large, ornate Bible with her everywhere, spooked the crew when a grip's arm was broken in an accident; she approached him and touched his arm, as if to heal it! She and the director had a bitter argument about how long her hair should be. Not long after that he received a package in the mail containing locks of Young's hair.

Once her relationship with Woods was cut off, she began acting even more strangely around the set, and Woods and Owen became the victims of a bizarre terror campaign. Someone—and Woods has always held that it was Young—trampled five hundred dollars worth of flowers in his garden; made threatening phone calls to him in the night; put Woods and Owen on antiabortion mailing lists (Owen had had an abortion); and mailed the couple pictures of mutilated corpses and animals. Worst of all was the doll Woods found on his step one night; the doll's throat had been cut and iodine had been poured on its chest to simulate blood. Its face had been painted white to resemble a corpse.

Woods filed a $6 million lawsuit against Young, who continues to maintain that she is innocent. Woods and Owen did marry, but divorced a short time later.

One begins to think Hollywood ain't big enough for the two of *any*body.

Reynolds used to audition for jobs with a monologue of Brando "look-alike" jokes. Perhaps Brando heard about it, because Reynolds was once dragged over to a table in a Los Angeles restaurant to meet the brooding actor. Brando turned away and spoke not a word to Reynolds, who was later quoted by the *National Enquirer* (a quote he has never retracted, by the way), claiming that Brando had "the mentality of an 11-year-old . . . when he's not acting, he's about as interesting to talk to as a wall safe." Perhaps Brando feels it's beneath him to strike back, as that was the last Hollywood heard of the simmering feud.

Perhaps the strangest feud in Hollywood, past or present, resulted from the failed offscreen romance between the two stars of the 1987 film

What I have crossed out I didn't like. What I haven't crossed out I am dissatisfied with.

— Cecil B. De Mille, his note on a script returned to a writer

CHAPTER EIGHT

Oscar Night

Since its inception over sixty years ago, the Academy of Motion Picture Arts and Sciences—and its annual awards ceremony—has grown in influence and importance, and today it stands for all that is Hollywood. One night every year—Oscar Night—the Academy sets out to award those it perceives as excellent in their profession, from actors and directors to costume designers. The Hollywood community, in turn, pulls out all the stops and—with the whole world watching—flashes all the glitz, glamour, and ego it can muster. Watching Oscar Night is like glimpsing Hollywood under a microscope, and it's the perfect opportunity to see how Tinseltown really works.

The Academy itself was the brainchild of Louis B. Mayer in 1927. Its purpose was twofold.

The twenties saw widespread unionism in America, and Mayer was getting nervous. He formed the Academy as a sort of management guild in an attempt to head off the looming threat of organized labor. Also, by this time, the great drug abuse and sex scandals of the twenties had rocked the industry to its very foundation, so Mayer felt the creation of a professional organization might lend the film industry a note of respectability.

The original charter for the organization was threadbare and made no mention of awards. When the Academy started presenting awards two years later (and on through the thirties), the winners were handpicked by a small group of studio heads presided over by Mayer. The purpose behind awards was simple: they were a

Opposite: Denzel Washington poses with his Oscar. Right: In 1941, the Academy virtually ignored Orson Welles' now-classic Citizen Kane.

politically driven public relations vehicle for the studios. The Academy limped along through the thirties—its membership was impoverished and the awards were perceived as little more than a gimmick. Hollow and ineffectual, the system reached its lowest point in 1941. That year *Citizen Kane* was without doubt the best picture of the year (contemporary critics often say the best American film ever made). But Orson Welles' mas-

terpiece—a thinly veiled portrait of the publishing giant and Hollywood power-monger William Randolph Hearst, who could make or break any studio in town—was too politically hot, so the Academy sidestepped the issue, ignoring one of the industry's crowning achievements. *How Green Was My Valley* won Best Picture that year.

The system has improved since that all-time low, but not by much. Nominees throughout the

Above: George C. Scott as Patton, the role for which he won—and refused—an Oscar in 1970. Opposite: John Wayne with Academy Award–winner Joanne Woodward, 1957.

SOME CINEMA NOTABLES WHO NEVER RECEIVED A NOMINATION

Lauren Bacall, Lucille Ball, John Barrymore, Lon Chaney, Noel Coward, Douglas Fairbanks (Jr. and Sr.), Mia Farrow, W. C. Fields, Errol Flynn, Jean Harlow, Rita Hayworth, Bob Hope, Danny Kaye, Alan Ladd, Veronica Lake, Peter Lorre, Myrna Loy, Fred MacMurray, Dick Powell, Tyrone Power, Ronald Reagan, Max Von Sydow, Mae West

Oscars' history have frequently taken the Academy to task, voicing concerns about the politics or policies of the awards or the appropriateness of actors, directors, and writers competing against one another. Often nominees would send such a message by having someone else go to receive the award in their stead.

But until 1970, when George C. Scott was nominated for his role in *Patton*, no one had ever declined an Oscar before. Scott explained his feelings toward the honor to the Associated Press. "The Academy Award show is a 'meat parade'," he said, "Life isn't a race. It's a war of survival . . . . I don't consider myself in competition with my fellow actors for rewards or recognition." He stated flatly that he rejected his nomination. The Academy, attracted to Scott's maverick attitude, gave him the award anyway. He refused to accept it.

It was Marlon Brando—always an intriguing and controversial figure—who combined the tried-and-true custom of sending a stand-in with refusing an award. He sent someone in his place to the 1972 Academy Awards, the year he was nominated for Best Actor for his performance in *The Godfather*.

The producers of the show were fully prepared for Brando not to show up. In fact, up until moments before the broadcast, Paramount pro-

ducer Robert Evans was set to accept for Brando. But just as the ceremony got under way, a woman calling herself Sacheen Littlefeather appeared with Brando's secretary, prepared to read a five-page speech should Brando win. The producers forbade her to read the speech but had no choice but to let her accept for Brando.

When Brando's name was called as the winner, Sacheen took the podium and declined the honor for Brando, citing his protest of the treatment of Native Americans in the United States in general, and by Hollywood, specifically. It was a moment the stunned audience would never forget. Brando had instantly established the Awards as a soapbox, an opportunity to air personal political opinions. The Oscars have never been the same since.

Sacheen Littlefeather was actually Maria Cruz, sometime bit actress, former Miss Vampire U.S.A., and full-time Native American activist. She had been corresponding with Brando about the plight of the American Indian for some time before he called her on the eve of the Awards ceremony and asked if she'd do him a favor.

A year later on television with Dick Cavett, Brando showed signs of regret. "Would I do it again?" he said, "Well, uh, I don't think so."

In 1974, a man named Robert Opal mysteriously managed to penetrate what had been considered the tightest possible security to air something completely different on an Oscar broadcast.

Somehow Opal managed to get hold of a yellow press pass and had used it to get by the many guards backstage. Once there, while David Niven prepared to introduce Elizabeth Taylor,

[An Academy
Award is] . . .
sort of a
popularity test.
When it's your
turn, you win it.

—Woody Allen

Above: **Rain Man** *costars* **Tom Cruise and Dustin Hoffman at the 1989 Academy Award ceremonies. Rain Man won three Oscars: Best Picture, Best Director, and Best Actor (Hoffman).**

Opal stripped naked behind a set piece of Oscar himself and "streaked" across the stage. The flustered Niven regained his composure and cracked, "Isn't it fascinating that probably the only laugh that man will ever get in his life is by stripping off his clothes and showing us his shortcomings."

Marty Pasetta, the director of that night's broadcast, later said, "I looked up [at the monitors] and saw him times six." He was able to tell two things about Opal. "The 'shortcomings' mentioned by David Niven were anything but . . . and he wasn't Jewish."

Opal was taken into custody while hurrying back into his tux backstage. His refusal to admit how he got a pass and the fact that the Academy's publicist told police to let him go fostered rumors that the stunt had been planned for publicity. Opal denied this. (An odd side note: Opal was killed in 1979 when his San Francisco sex paraphernalia shop was robbed.)

Rodeo Drive, the chic shopping street in Beverly Hills, is said to have two seasons: Christmas and Oscar month. The Awards ceremony and parties (not to mention the numerous social events in the weeks preceding the actual night) have become a virtual fashion battleground where anything goes.

Star apparel has been important on Oscar Night since the earliest presentations. Mary Pickford ordered her gown from Paris the same week she began work on *Coquette*, the picture she planned to win the Oscar with. She had the luxury of time because back in those days an actress of Pickford's stature could use her clout to secure an Oscar as soon as she signed a contract for a particular film.

The Academy Awards were transformed into a fashion World Series with the first televised Oscar broadcast in 1953. Suddenly millions of fans would be able to scrutinize each star's every movement and true proportions.

With such pressures bearing down on her, Joan Crawford once asked Edith Head—for years the primary Oscar wardrobe designer—to design for her one black dress and one white, just in case a rival of hers appeared on stage in the same color before Joan went out to present. She was lucky to have such foresight that particular year; she needed the extra gown and was, as Head recalled, "the hit of the evening."

But Oscar Night wasn't the fashion free-for-all it is now until the 1985 awards—the year Cher was passed over in the nomination process for her work in *Mask*.

That year, the Academy nominated Anne Bancroft for what critics called "a hammy, dated, stagey" performance of a nun in *Agnes of God*. Cher felt justifiably betrayed and the moment she learned of the nominations she got her designer, Bob Mackie, on the phone, and called a huddle in her New York penthouse. Cher gave Mackie an edict for her dress that year: "They didn't nominate me this year so f— it . . . to hell with it!" said Cher. "Let's have some fun!" The designer said he decided to give the Academy "a good ride."

What a ride it was! Mackie created an incredibly revealing, wildly fantastic dress, made of a fabric covered in beads shipped from the Third World. The crowning glory was a feathered headdress with eight hundred nine-inch (23-cm) hackles plucked from only the largest wild French roosters. Cher also wore thigh-high boots made of the best Spanish leather.

As Cher strode out to present the award to the Best Supporting Actor (Don Ameche, that year), the audience was truly stunned. "As you can see," she said from the stage, "I have received and read my Academy brochure on how to dress as a *serious* actress."

Cher's dress was the high point of the evening that year—and perhaps even that decade. Ah, sweet revenge!

Below: Cher, scorned by the Academy, decided to "have some fun" on the Oscar broadcast. Following pages: The scene outside the 40th Annual Academy Awards.

OSCAR ODDITIES

After Spencer Tracy won his 1937 Oscar for *Captains Courageous*, the statuette was sent out to be inscribed. It was finally returned to the actor—much to the embarrassment of the Academy—engraved "To Dick Tracy."

Two years before declining his Oscar for *The Godfather* in 1971, Marlon Brando applied to the Academy for a replacement of the Oscar statuette he had won for *On the Waterfront* in 1954, which had been stolen.

Woody Allen was unable to attend the Academy Awards ceremony in 1977 to pick up the three Oscars he won for *Annie Hall* because he had a regular Monday night gig playing clarinet at a Manhattan jazz club and chose not to let the band down.

France, perhaps the most cinematic country in the world, resisted broadcasting the Academy Awards on television until 1986.

SHORT BUT MEMORABLE OSCAR ACCEPTANCE SPEECHES

I should have put on that eye patch a long time ago.
—John Wayne, Best Actor,
True Grit, 1969

I accept this very gratefully for keeping my mouth shut. I think I'll do it again.
—Jane Wyman,
Best Actress,
(she played a deaf mute)
Johnny Belinda, 1948

I'm going to take it home and design a dress for it.
— Edith Head,
Best Costume Design,
Roman Holiday, 1953

I think half of this belongs to a horse somewhere out in the Valley.
— Lee Marvin,
Best Actor,
Cat Ballou, 1965

Hello, gorgeous.
— Barbara Streisand,
Best Actress,
Funny Girl, 1968

I'm thrilled, happy, delighted . . . sober!
— Maureen Stapleton,
Best Supporting Actress,
Reds, 1981

Holy mackerel!
— Meryl Streep,
Best Supporting Actress,
Kramer vs. Kramer, 1979

THE ACADE

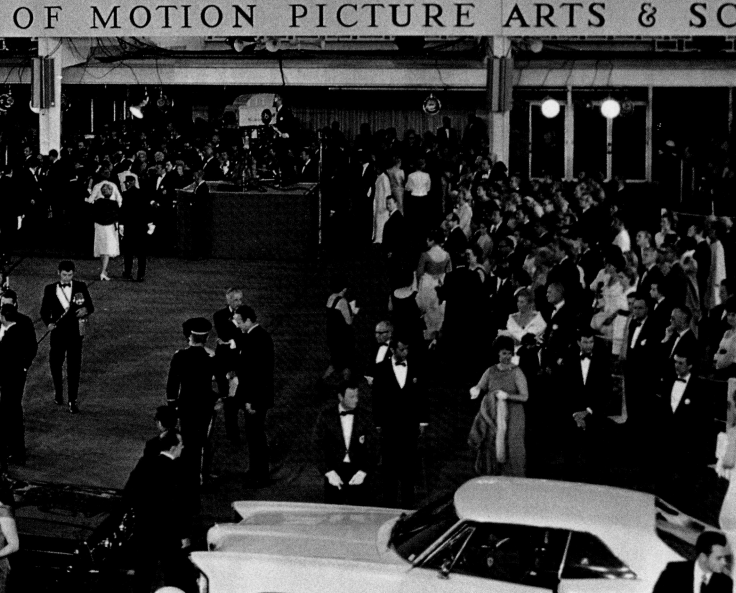

40TH ANNUAL ACADEMY AWARDS

OF MOTION PICTURE ARTS & SC

The year you win an Oscar is the fastest year in a Hollywood actor's life. Twelve months later they ask— "Who won the Oscar last year?"

— Cliff Robertson

True Grit

part four

CHAPTER NINE

Scandal!

As we have seen, Hollywood movie stars, basking in instant riches, fame, and glamour have always lived their lives, especially their sex lives, outside the usual boundaries of society. During their reign, the major studios—needing the stars as much as the stars needed them—spent a lot of money and energy to keep the wild behavior of their contract players out of the public eye. But once in a while, something would happen that was so wicked, titillating, or depraved that even the best studio public relations people just couldn't keep a lid on it. That's pure scandal.

Hollywood has been virtually synonymous with scandal since 1921, the year America's most beloved chubby comedian raped a popular starlet; the act resulted in her death days later.

That year, Roscoe "Fatty" Arbuckle was thirty-four years old, weighed in at over three hundred pounds (136 kg), and was second only to the great Charlie Chaplin at America's box offices. Arbuckle ate huge amounts of food, drank vast quantities of bathtub gin, and was renowned for giving raucous parties. Even more so than all these other vices, his true passion was sex. The man may have been fat, but he was *very* rich and world-famous and had no trouble attracting women.

Arbuckle had set his sights on young Virginia Rappe and had been pursuing her for several years. She had not responded to his overtures. Rappe, whose wholesome face adorned the sheet music to the biggest hit of the day, "Let Me Call You Sweetheart," was involved with director

Henri Lehrman at the time and continually rebuffed Arbuckle's advances. Nevertheless, Arbuckle, through a third person, managed to invite her to a party he was throwing to celebrate his recent signing of a $3 million contract.

The party started early in the day at the staid St. Francis Hotel in San Francisco—the largest metropolis within driving distance of Hollywood at the time and, consequently, a popular playground for filmdom's elite. As the day wore on, the Hollywood crowd grew drunk and boisterous. At one point Arbuckle led the very drunk Rappe into the bedroom and locked the door behind them. Sometime later, the other guests heard Rappe screaming. They tried, but were unable, to open the locked door; someone went to get the hotel manager. Before the manager could open the door, Arbuckle did so himself and stood smiling in the doorway, still dressed as he had been all day—in his bathrobe and slippers. Guests ran into the room to find Rappe writhing in pain, naked on the bed. Her clothes, ripped to shreds, lay about the room. Several women at the party made attempts to calm her; an ice-cold bath meant to sooth her only made her suffering worse. Arbuckle was certain the woman was faking her discomfort.

The party broke up, and Arbuckle returned to Hollywood. A doctor was called in to treat Rappe; two days passed before it was determined she needed more intensive medical treatment. She was moved to a hospital.

Over the next few days, Rappe passed in and out of consciousness. During one lucid moment, she worried about paying her medical bills, telling a nurse that Arbuckle should pay because "he did this to me." She died the next day from an internal infection caused by a burst bladder. The San Francisco coroner ruled that Arbuckle's great weight had burst the woman's bladder during the attempted rape.

The San Francisco District Attorney was intent on convicting the actor for manslaughter. Three highly publicized trials followed. The first jury was unable to reach a majority to convict him. The second jury yielded a mistrial as well. In April

1922, a third jury found Arbuckle innocent. There were rumors that Arbuckle's studio had paid off important officials and thus affected the outcome of the trial.

After the verdict was read, Arbuckle announced, "My innocence of the hideous charge . . . has been proved." Maybe so, but even before the first trial had ended, Arbuckle had been convicted—by moviegoers. Their image of the cherubic, innocent, roly-poly clown was gone forever, marred by headlines associating him with rape and death.

Arbuckle's $3 million contract was canceled, his unreleased films suppressed (at a cost of $1 million to the studio). The comedian languished,

Opposite: Lana Turner on the witness stand explaining how her daughter stabbed and killed her lover Johnny Stompanato. Above: Fatty Arbuckle and Mabel Normand ham it up.

unemployable for years, while pleading with the industry to let him work. In 1933, at the age of forty-six, it seemed he would finally get a second chance when Warner Brothers hired him to make some short comedies. But since his debacle he'd done little but drink, and the toll the alcohol took was too great. After attending a party in New York celebrating his return to movies, Arbuckle retired to his hotel room and died of a heart attack.

The other great comedian of the day, Charlie Chaplin, was lucky to barely escape Fatty Arbuckle's fate. Chaplin, too, was dogged by scandal his entire career in Hollywood, but somehow he managed to stay one step ahead of it—for a time.

The brilliant actor-director had a troubled love life. It has been said that his almost painful shyness drew him to very young women. His first love was Mildred Harris, whom he met at a beach party in 1917. The girl was only fifteen, and she looked even younger; Chaplin was twenty-eight. They became involved a year later. When she announced that she was pregnant, the couple married immediately in order to avoid a charge of statutory rape; they divorced two years later.

Chaplin's next serious involvement was with Lolita McMurray, whom he met when she was six

years old. When she was twelve, he cast her as a child angel in *The Kid*. McMurray's mother was suspicious of Chaplin from the start and kept a close watch on him. Two years later, in 1922, Chaplin cast Lolita in *The Gold Rush*, the classic he filmed in Truckee, California. It was there that the thirty-two-year-old Chaplin vigorously pursued the girl (her personal account would indicate that he virtually raped her several times), eventually winning her over. She, too, became pregnant, and they were quickly married. The girl and her mother promptly took up residence in Chaplin's Hollywood mansion.

Two years later, Chaplin fled to New York and Lolita filed for divorce. According to *Scandal!*, by Colin Wilson and Donald Seaman, her allegations—that he made her perform "abnormal, against nature, perverted, degenerate and inde-

Left: Mildred Harris Chaplin in The Inferior Sex, *1920. Above: Lolita McMurray Chaplin.*

cent acts"—were made public, and the press had a field day at Chaplin's expense. Lolita's lawyers threatened to release the names of five prominent actresses with whom Chaplin had engaged in sex *since* his marriage. Chaplin had no choice but to capitulate, paying $65,000 to Lolita and her mother (which he could well afford; at the time he was worth $16 million). Chaplin was so embittered by the case that Lolita does not even appear in his autobiography. Oddly, the publicity surrounding the nasty divorce did not harm his movie career. *The Circus*, Chaplin's next film, was as popular as ever.

Scandal, however, continued to dog Chaplin. In 1942 he was the defendant in a paternity suit filed by a young actress named Joan Barry and was found to be the child's father. Later, during the McCarthy era, Chaplin was accused of being a Communist and was threatened by the United States government with an inquiry into his "moral worth"; Chaplin took up residence in Switzerland from that day until his death in 1977.

The juicy Hollywood sex scandals of the 1920s left fans hungry for more. The 1930s brought along a big dose of adultery—described in a film star's own words—when Dr. Franklyn Thorpe discovered his wife's diary in an underwear drawer. Upon opening the diary, his eyes fell on the words:

. . . remarkable staying power; I don't know how he does it.

The diary belonged to actress Mary Astor. The man with "remarkable staying power" turned out to be playwright George S. Kaufman, who coauthored the Marx Brothers' film *A Night At the Opera* and was himself a married man.

Thorpe begged his wife to end the affair that she so graphically detailed in the diary and come back to him. She refused. Instead she packed her bags and moved out; divorce proceedings were begun. The judge in the case refused to allow the diary to be read aloud in court (in fact, he later ordered to have it burned), but Dr. Thorpe's lawyers managed to leak key passages to the press, hoping to win public approval for their client and a better chance of his winning the child custody battle. The press, of course, was only too happy to reprint them—with all the offending words blacked out.

Soon all of America was treated to a steamy tale of adultery in Astor's own lusty prose (much of it reprinted today in Kenneth Anger's entertaining *Hollywood Babylon*). They learned how, after meeting Kaufman for the first time in New York, they went to the theater where, Astor wrote, "my hand wasn't in my own lap . . . It's been years since I felt up a man in public, but I just got carried away." She confessed to retreating to Kaufman's small apartment on Seventy-third Street where they settled into hours of lovemaking. Astor wrote: "His powers of recooperation [sic] are amazing, and we made love all night long." The lovers made frequent trips to the apartment where, she revealed, "he f—ed the living daylights out of me." They took a trip to Palm Springs and Astor recorded it all in the diary. Newspapers printed the result, including the infamous quote: "Ah, desert night—with George's body plunging into mine, naked under the stars."

It looked as if Mary Astor's career was finished—she'd even made plans to go to work as a buyer at a womenswear store. But, luckily for Astor, her screen image was not that of a pure and innocent virgin (and it never had been), so the publicity did little to hurt her career. In fact, after the diary was made public, audiences stood and cheered when she appeared on screen. Her acting career continued, unhindered, on into the sixties.

Perhaps it is no surprise that the biggest Hollywood sex scandal to follow whirled around the amorous Errol Flynn.

Below: Steamy diarist Mary Astor.

It isn't what they say about you— it's what they whisper about you.

—Errol Flynn

Opposite: The king of the Hollywood playboys, Errol Flynn, relaxes at home.

In September 1942, Flynn attended a garden party in Bel Air. A group of teenagers arrived, led by a young man named Armand Knapp, a studio messenger boy. One of the group was Knapp's girlfriend, Betty Hansen. Betty began drinking heavily and took to sitting on Flynn's lap while he continued to talk to others over the top of the girl's head. At dinner Hansen announced that she was going to be sick; Flynn walked her up to a bedroom and told her to lie down and get some sleep. According to Hansen, Flynn removed her clothing—she said she believed he was tucking her into bed—and then removed his own. He proceeded to have sex with her for half an hour.

Afterward, while Flynn showered, one of Hansen's friends took her home, where she told her sister that Flynn had seduced her. She was taken into protective custody at Juvenile Hall, and the District Attorney was notified.

The District Attorney at the time recalled a similar case some fourteen months earlier where another seventeen-year-old, Peggy Satterlee, claimed that Flynn had raped her on his yacht. The District Attorney, eager to prove that Hollywood and its stars were not above the law, saw a chance to try Flynn on both counts and hopefully get a conviction. In January 1943, Flynn appeared in court, defended by the brilliant celebrity lawyer Jerry Giesler.

Giesler was quickly able to get Betty Hansen to contradict her original testimony on the stand. He also got her to admit that at the time she'd been "raped" by Flynn, she was already in trouble with Juvenile authorities for committing an act of oral sex on her boyfriend Knapp.

Next to testify was Peggy Satterlee. She claimed that, while on a trip aboard Flynn's yacht, Flynn had entered her cabin on the first night, crawled into her bed, and had intercourse with her—after which he brought her a glass of milk. The next night, she testified, Flynn invited her to his cabin to "see the moon through a porthole." Once she was there, Flynn insisted that since he had possessed her the previous night there was no reason he should not have her again. He forcibly had intercourse with her that second

FOR THE LOVE OF MONEY

Befitting a time now regarded as the "greed decade," a few of the more notable Hollywood scandals during the late seventies and early eighties had a definite financial bent. For the first time in Hollywood's history, headlines screamed more about boardrooms than bedrooms, and more about money than sex and drugs. Here are two classic stories that mirror the times.

The Begelman Affair

David Begelman, president of Columbia Pictures in 1977, had a problem. It seems he had a habit of asking the studio treasurer to cut $10,000 checks for some unsuspecting technician or actor—say, Cliff Robertson. Begelman would then endorse the check himself and pocket the cash—in other words, commit a felony. Robertson received a tax statement about earnings he'd never seen and began an inquiry. The resulting power struggle on the lot and in the boardroom of Columbia over Begelman's fate, a valuable creative resource, nearly toppled the great studio. In the end, Begelman received a legal slap on the wrist and, after a short stint as an independent producer with a deal at Columbia, was once again the president of a major studio, first MGM and then United Artists. For his role in the matter, Cliff Robertson was virtually blacklisted for four years.

Heaven's Gate

Oscar-winning director, Michael Cimino, had a vision, a western he wanted to make, called *Heaven's Gate*. Executives at United Artists—a historic studio begun by Chaplin, Griffith, Fairbanks, and Pickford with high ideals about creative license for artists—decided to fund the project.

Cimino went to Montana to shoot and became entrenched there, shooting millions and millions of dollars worth of film, lagging far behind schedule, and ignoring the pleas of studio executives who clamored for him to pull the picture together and keep a lid on the budget. Before it was over, Cimino spent $44 million and eventually handed over a two-and-a-half-hour film that, although strikingly photographed, was nearly impossible to sit through.

The 1980 film was a critical and box-office flop (one of the biggest in history), and the financial strain weakened United Artists to the extent that it was dismantled and merged into MGM/UA almost before anyone at the studio knew what had happened.

night, despite her struggle and insistence that she hurt from their encounter the night before. Her testimony, corroborated by a police doctor, was condemning. But Giesler made public the fact that in the year following the rape the girl had an abortion, then an illegal procedure, and was still under the charge. His aim was clear; he hoped to imply that both girls were looking for leniency from the police in exchange for their Flynn rape testimonies.

Flynn, on the witness stand, denied ever having slept with either girl (although in his autobiography, *My Wicked, Wicked Ways*, he admits to sleeping with Satterlee—and omits Hansen altogether). Eventually, the jury found him not guilty. Warner Brothers was more than relieved—their swashbuckling star had been vindicated. Even more, the scandalous trial actually seemed to increase Flynn's popularity; his next films, *Desperate Journey* and *Gentleman Jim*, played to packed theaters.

It would take more than just sex to cause a scandal in Hollywood after that, for America after World War II had a tougher hide. It would take a sex scandal with murder thrown into the mix to really grab the headlines. That's what the public got with the death of Lana Turner's boyfriend, Johnny Stompanato.

Turner's career began in her teens when a journalist spotted her as she was playing hooky from school, sitting in a malt shop (legend has it she was in the famous Schwab's Drugstore in Hollywood), wearing a tight sweater. Soon after, she appeared in *They Won't Forget*. She quickly became known as the "Sweater Girl," a favorite GI pinup during World War II.

Turner's love life was a bouncy one. She married band leader Artie Shaw; the marriage lasted two months. She met her second husband, Stephen Crane, when he asked her to dance on a bet; they were married nine days later. Husband number three was playboy millionaire Bob Topping. Husband number four was movie Tarzan Lex Barker. In between assorted husbands, she dated the likes of Frank Sinatra, Howard Hughes, Tyrone Power, and Fernando Lamas.

Turner had split with Barker and her career was floundering when she met Johnny Stompanato, another man who approached her on a bet.

Stompanato was the ex-bodyguard of gangster Mickey Cohen. He lied to Turner, telling her he was ten years older than she, when he was actually years younger. He wore silk shirts open to his belt to show off his chest hair. He was also nicknamed Oscar—for a vital part of his anatomy that was just about the size of an Oscar statuette when upright. Whatever his appeal to Turner, the relationship became an instant—and mutual—obsession.

Both Turner and Stompanato had strong personalities, so the two would often clash. Once, unable to stay away from her for long, Stompanato borrowed money for a flight to London where Turner was making a movie with Sean Connery. He was deported days later by British police after threatening to slash Turner's face with a razor during an argument.

On Friday, April 4, 1958, not long after the London incident, Stompanato and Turner had another violent argument, this time in her Beverly Hills home. Cheryl—Turner's daughter by her second husband—heard the noisy quarrel and feared for her mother's safety. She ran to the kitchen, grabbed a carving knife, and went to see if her mother was all right. When Cheryl first appeared, Turner asked her to go away, telling her everything was fine. Moments later, Turner began to scream, and Cheryl heard Stompanato threatening to disfigure or cripple her mother. She opened the door to her mother's room again and saw Stompanato swinging at her mother with a jacket on a hanger. She rushed toward him and seemed to hit him in the stomach. He fell to the floor with a knife wound in his abdomen.

A doctor was summoned, but there was nothing he could do. The knife had slashed through Stompanato's aorta; he was dead within

Above:
"The Sweater Girl," Lana Turner.

minutes. Los Angeles police chief Clinton B. Anderson was summoned as well; he arrived to find attorney Jerry Giesler already at the scene!

The trial was big news. Turner shed tears on the witness stand and eventually won over the jury, who ruled the death a justifiable homicide. Stompanato's brother filed a lawsuit against Cheryl's parents, claiming $800,000 for parental negligence. The claim was settled out of court for $20,000.

If any scandal would seem to hold the promise of damaging a career, this was it. And yet, miraculously, even murder didn't seem to be too much. Turner's career revived dramatically after the trial. During showings of *Another Time, Another Place*—the movie she had made in London with Connery—people stood and shouted their support. The scandal proved to be as good as any publicity stunt and signaled that the age of Hollywood scandal was essentially over. If murder couldn't shock, what could? The next two decades were free of outright scandal—if not the usual wicked gossip (much of it recorded in these pages)—until 1977 when Hollywood seemed to have been yanked right back to the Golden Age.

Roman Polanski, the Polish director of films such as *Rosemary's Baby* and *Chinatown*, had a self-admitted attraction to underage girls. It was this attraction which, in 1977, led him to suggest an article about adolescent girls for *Vogue* magazine to be accompanied by a series of photographs. The magazine hired Polanski to

shoot the pictures. It was while working on this assignment that he met a thirteen-year-old actress-model at the home of the girl's mother.

According to Polanski, he and the girl left the house and went out to shoot pictures in the Hollywood hills. One of the locations was Jacqueline Bisset's home—but the lighting there was wrong. They crossed Mulholland Drive to the home of Jack Nicholson. Nicholson wasn't home, but his girlfriend at the time, Anjelica Huston, let the twosome in to shoot pictures around the pool and Jacuzzi.

The girl eventually stripped naked and, while Polanski clicked away, began to tell him about the sex she had with her boyfriend. Soon Polanski, too, was naked and in the hot tub with the girl. They moved inside and made love on the couch. As he later wrote in his autobiography, *Roman*, "there could be no doubt about Sandra's experience and lack of inhibition." Afterward, he drove the girl home, smoked a joint with her mother, and said his good-byes.

The next day Polanski was arrested in his hotel lobby.

Between his trial and his sentencing, Polanski was kept in Chino prison in California for forty-

Left: Lana Turner's daughter Cheryl Crane being booked for the murder of Johnny Stompanato. Below: Roman Polanski in Cannes with his eighteen-year-old girlfriend, Nastassja Kinski, in 1979.

two days. The judge on the case had been hinting at giving Polanski another forty-two days in prison and then deporting him. Taking the hint, Polanski borrowed $5,000 from producer Dino De Laurentiis and hopped a plane to London, then to France. He has not returned to the United States since. He has continued to date very young women, including Nastassja Kinski—who was eighteen at the time of their relationship—and his current wife, Emmanuelle Seigner, whom he met when she was nineteen.

Hollywood's casual drug use of the seventies blossomed into full-fledged drug abuse in the eighties. This fact was brought to light by the sudden and tragic death of John Belushi in 1982—a death that threatened to spread drug scandal throughout the Hollywood community and bring on another round of federal witch-hunts to attempt to clean up Hollywood.

Belushi, the beefy star of *National Lampoon's Animal House* and *The Blues Brothers*, spent most of his time in New York where he lived with his wife, Judy. But he made frequent short trips to Hollywood, where he would rent his favorite bungalow at the rundown Chateau Marmont Hotel on Sunset Boulevard for $200 a day. There he would take meetings, work with other writers, and party with an ever-widening circle of "friends," all Hollywood drug users.

Below: Dan Ackroyd and John Belushi in **The Blues Brothers, 1980.**

In March 1982, things were going badly for Belushi. He was working on a film script based on the bestseller *The Joy of Sex.* Michael Eisner, then head of Paramount, was unhappy with his work, telling him it needed a major rewrite; at the same time, the studio was putting a lot of pressure on him to make the film a smash hit. Under the tension, Belushi would often resort to self-destructive behavior. On the night of March 4, 1982, he took that behavior one step too far.

Belushi spent most of that day with Cathy Evelyn Smith, a former backup singer and somewhat of a movie star groupie. Smith provided Belushi with his first speedball that day—a mixture of cocaine and heroin that is injected. They drove around all day, shooting up, scoring more drugs, and arranging to meet a group of friends for a party in Belushi's bungalow that night.

By the time the two got back to the hotel that night, Smith had to help Belushi from the car into the bungalow. He felt ill and was vomiting as his friends began arriving. Comedian Robin Williams left shortly after he got there, feeling uncomfortable about Belushi's fading in and out of consciousness. Actor Robert De Niro also made a brief appearance, but left after snorting a few lines of coke.

Belushi complained of feeling cold. Smith shot up, then gave Belushi another speedball; they eventually went to sleep. Smith says she left Belushi snoring loudly the next morning at 10:00 A.M. so that she could place a bet on a horse. At noon, when Belushi's personal trainer arrived at the room, he found Belushi huddled in a fetal position under the blankets. The star was dead from the effects of the drugs at thirty-three.

The most recent Hollywood scandal once again involved the sex life of a star, but this time the evidence was even more condemning than a diary or even an eyewitness. This time the whole sordid event was recorded on videotape.

Actor Rob Lowe achieved fame as a screen idol. He was an integral member of what became known as the "Brat Pack," a tight-knit group of attractive young actors and actresses brought into the limelight in movies like *The Outsiders, The*

FAN-ATICS!

Avid fans are one thing, but some go too far:
Stephen Stillbower crashed a truck through the gates of Madonna and Sean Penn's Malibu home and roamed around the property for hours until Penn and sheriff's deputies caught him.

A female fan once climbed onto the roof of Tom Selleck's beach house and tried to climb in a window. The naked actor, roused from sleep, managed to scare her off.

An obsessive forty-three-year-old Michigan man sent more than two hundred threatening letters to actress Stephanie Zimbalist, claiming that one day he would thwart her continual "efforts to avoid him."

Nathan Trupp, believing Michael Landon to be a Nazi, shot and killed two Universal Studio guards in an attempt to hunt down and kill Landon on the lot.

Breakfast Club, and *St. Elmo's Fire*. Lowe was known as a ladies' man and had been linked romantically with Princess Stephanie of Monaco, actresses Melissa Gilbert and Nastassja Kinski, and even former National Security Council secretary Fawn Hall. But his voracious sex life nearly brought his career to a grinding halt.

Lowe had become politically active, having been recruited in 1985 by Senator Tom Hayden (Jane Fonda's ex-husband) to lend his celebrity power to the Democratic party. For that reason, Lowe was in Atlanta, Georgia, in July 1989 for the Democratic National Convention, where he was hoping to learn more about candidate Michael Dukakis. Lowe later told *Interview* magazine, " . . . conventions are, by nature, a party." And party he did, spending time drinking and dancing at Atlanta's wildest nightspot, Club Rio, where sources say the drug Ecstasy—a sexual stimulant—was widely used.

An hour after his arrival at Club Rio, Lowe left with two pretty young women. They went to his hotel, drank a few beers (Lowe offered cocaine, but the girls declined), and began having sex. As an added kick, Lowe set up his video camera to record the evening's activities (an old, well-known hobby of Lowe's, say friends).

During a break in the action, Lowe went into the bathroom. When he came out, he found that the girls had left and had taken that revealing video tape with them.

A month later, Lowe received word that he had been served with a civil suit by the mother of one of the girls, whose daughter, Jan Parsons, happened to be sixteen at the time of the event. The mother's suit, according to *Interview*, charged Lowe with using "his celebrity status as an inducement to females to engage in sexual intercourse, sodomy, and multiple-partner sexual activity for his immediate sexual gratification, and for the purpose of making pornographic films of these activities."

The suit stirred up a criminal investigation of Lowe by the Fulton County District Attorney, who sought to charge Lowe with sexually exploiting a minor to produce pornography. Lowe's lawyers

bargained with the District Attorney; Lowe had to perform twenty hours of public service work in Los Angeles and in his hometown, Dayton, Ohio, in exchange for dropping the charges.

The jury is still out on whether the scandal hurt Lowe's image or Hollywood "bankability." A screenwriter was quoted anonymously in *People* saying, "It could give Rob an edge, take away from that too-perfect image and make him more intriguing." As far as Lowe's political future is concerned, the situation looks less rosy. Bob Oettinger, whose Celebrity Outreach Foundation hooks up stars with various causes, says, "Rob wouldn't get a visible role in a political campaign today. He might be allowed to lick envelopes."

But once again, scandal may turn out to be a public relations boon for a Hollywood star. It would seem that any potentially shocking behavior that doesn't result in a star's death will probably end up advancing his or her career. The old show business axiom "there's no such thing as bad publicity" continues to hold true.

Above: Rob Lowe and former flame, actress Melissa Gilbert, 1986.

CHAPTER TEN

Unsolved Hollywood Mysteries

Raised above gossip and scandal by the questions they left unanswered, a handful of enduring Hollywood mysteries—even those whose principal players have long since faded into obscurity—continue to fascinate the public.

Before Fatty Arbuckle had been acquitted of raping Virginia Rappe in April 1922 (see page 136), another scandal broke over the hypersensitized Hollywood community that year, when director William Desmond Taylor was found shot to death in his Hollywood bungalow.

Taylor was one of the most successful of the early directors at Famous Players-Lasky (which later became Paramount). A man of some education, he stood out in the Hollywood crowd and drew women like a magnet. Among his many lovers were two actresses, Mabel Normand and Mary Miles Minter. Minter's mother, Charlotte Selby, was a lover of his as well.

Mabel Normand and Taylor's butler Henry Peavey were the last to see him alive the night of the shooting. Peavey found Taylor's body the next morning; Taylor was lying serenely on his back in the center of the living room, his arms resting at his sides, his hair neatly combed. (It was later discovered that the bullet holes in his coat and his body didn't match up, which suggested that he'd had his arms up when he was shot.) After Peavey found his boss, he ran out into the courtyard shouting, "Mr. Taylor is dead! Mr. Taylor is dead!"

Word quickly spread. Normand, Minter, and Selby rushed to the scene before the police or coroner could arrive. They were soon joined by

studio executives who, well aware of Taylor's many and varied lovers, were dispatched to retrieve any condemning evidence, for the last thing Hollywood needed at the time was another sex scandal. The women likewise were intent on recovering love letters and lingerie that might connect them with the dead man.

The coroner walked in to find this crowd of people rummaging about the scene of the crime. Once everyone had been dispersed, police managed to find love letters from Normand (hidden in the dead director's boots), a frilly pink nightgown monogrammed with the initials 'M.M.M.,' and steamy letters signed "Love, Mary." The police also uncovered a secret stash of women's undergarments of all sizes, shapes, and colors, as well as photographs of Taylor engaged in sexual acts with a number of female stars.

The ensuing scandal hit the papers and brought an immediate end to Mabel Normand's career—her monthly $2,000 cocaine habit and connections to notorious drug dealers were uncovered and made public during the investigation. Mary Miles Minter's career, too, was snuffed out. A competitor of "Little" Mary Pickford, Minter's true age was revealed to be thirty, not twenty as her publicity machine had maintained. That fact and her lustful connection to a forty-five-year-old depraved man ruined her sweet, young, and innocent image for good.

Minter was so overcome at Taylor's funeral that she threw herself on the open casket and kissed the corpse on the lips. She then turned and announced that the dead man had whispered, "I shall always love you, Mary."

The investigation turned up interesting facts about Taylor as well. Taylor had once been known as William Cunningham Deane-Tanner, a successful art connoisseur in New York, who one day just up and vanished, taking $500 and a change of clothes, leaving behind a wife and daughter. He went to Hollywood and acted for a few years before going off to fight in World War I in the Canadian Army. He then returned to Hollywood a self-proclaimed director.

A prime suspect in the killing has always been Charlotte Selby, Mary Miles Minter's headstrong stage mother. Some say she tried to force a marriage between her daughter and Taylor, while others maintain that she was murderously jealous of their relationship. The fact is, little evidence exists to support any theory, thanks to the powerful studio executives who acted quickly to suppress the true story in an attempt to avoid scandal. Reportedly, the great director King Vidor came close to solving the

Opposite: William Desmond Taylor. His 1922 murder is still unsolved. Left: Charlotte Selby, mother of actress Mary Miles Minter (below), answers questions about Taylor's murder fifteen years after the fact.

Left: Happy loving couple Jean Harlow and producer Paul Bern tie the knot.

mystery while researching a film on the subject for Paramount in the sixties. It is said he learned the identity of the killer and then mysteriously shelved the project, possibly under pressure from the studio. The question of who killed William Desmond Taylor remains unanswered today.

The scandal stirred up by the Fatty Arbuckle rape trials and the William Desmond Taylor killing were instrumental in Hollywood's establishing the Hays Office to oversee conduct in the film capital and in the movies it made, effectively clamping down a tight lid on bad publicity. Ten years passed before another lonely death in Los Angeles focused world attention on Hollywood's seamier side. But then came the Paul Bern–Jean Harlow scandal of 1932.

Paul Bern was the quiet, unassuming assistant to Irving Thalberg at MGM. Although he was timid, Bern boldly set his romantic sights on Hollywood's biggest sex goddess at the time, Jean Harlow, and managed to woo her by driving her over to see his home. Sitting beside the swimming pool that first night, he impressed her by spending the entire evening talking about wine, and treating the blonde bombshell as if she had a brain. "He's different," she once said, "and he doesn't talk f—, f—, f— all the time." They were married two months later.

Three months after that, on September 5, 1932, Paul Bern shot himself in the head while standing naked before a mirror. He left an infamously cryptic note behind:

> Unfortunately this is the only way to make good the frightful wrong I have done you and wipe out my frightful humiliation.
>
> Paul
>
> P.S. You understand last night was only a comedy.

Eventually, it was learned that the night before his death Bern had walked into the bedroom he shared with Harlow wearing an enormous strap-on phallus. Harlow had burst into laughter when she saw the device, and Bern joined in. Together they slashed the leather

R.I.P. HOLLYWOOD

Montgomery Clift survived a horrible, disfiguring automobile accident only to permanently lose his striking good looks and self-confidence. His career waning, he died alone in bed, wearing only a pair of glasses, of a heart attack on July 22, 1966.

Princess Grace of Monaco, the former Grace Kelly, died after she sustained massive injuries in a car accident; her family asked that she be taken off of life-support systems in 1982.

Leslie Howard died when his civilian DC-3 was shot down over the Bay of Biscay by German fighters in the spring of 1943. The Germans may have thought the plane carried Winston Churchill.

Bruce Lee, the martial arts legend and near-perfect physical specimen, died on

July 20, 1973, from a heart attack brought on by an allergic reaction to painkillers he had been taking.

Vivien Leigh succumbed to tuberculosis and suffocated in her sleep on July 8, 1967.

Jayne Mansfield, her career fading, was decapitated when her car collided with a mosquito spray truck on June 29, 1967.

Audie Murphy, the most decorated soldier in World War II and the star of his filmed biography, *The Audie Murphy Story*, died in a plane crash on May 28, 1971.

George Reeves, television's Superman, excused himself from his houseguests, went to his bedroom, and shot himself on June 16, 1959. He was said to have been distraught over being typecast as "the Superman type."

member to bits with a pair of scissors and flushed the pieces down the toilet. According to Harlow's agent and closest friend at the time, Arthur Landau, Bern was impotent and had intended to satisfy his beautiful wife by artificial means. Landau suggested this was the "frightful wrong" Bern referred to.

But Bern's brother, Henry, has since offered a more interesting explanation—and perhaps a more plausible one.

Bern had previously lived for about five years in New York City's Algonquin Hotel with another attractive blonde, Dorothy Millette, who was known at the time as Mrs. Paul Bern. She had suffered a nervous breakdown and was sent to a Connecticut sanitarium. Her condition was pronounced "uncurable." Bern made arrangements for her to remain there and went on with his life.

Years later, miraculously, Millette recovered. Upon her release, she discovered that her husband was now married to screen star Jean Harlow. She wrote Bern and told him she was coming to California.

The evening before Bern's death, neighbors heard sounds of an argument coming from somewhere near Bern's swimming pool; others claim to have seen a limousine with a veiled woman in back in the vicinity. Henry Bern theorized that Millette arrived at the house and there had been a quarrel. Perhaps she threatened to publicly denounce Bern's "wrong"—his marriage to Harlow. After living with Bern for five years, Millette could have filed suit for bigamy.

To add an even stranger twist to the tale, the day after Bern's death, Millette boarded a riverboat steamer in San Francisco and, en route to Sacramento, threw herself overboard.

Years later, rumors and theories developed that perhaps Bern had not committed suicide, but that Millette had murdered him and that MGM executives forged the suicide note to protect Harlow from a bigamy scandal. (This may not be so farfetched—Louis B. Mayer himself was the first on the scene and supposedly pocketed the note before police arrived. He later walked back into the house to "return" the note to police.)

Again, MGM's incredible power in Hollywood kept Harlow away from the heat of scandal, and her reputation was barely singed.

But Hollywood was unable to protect Thelma Todd, another beautiful blonde comedienne of the time, who died a mysterious, cold, and lonely death just a few years later, in 1935.

Todd was a former beauty-queen-turned-sixth-grade-teacher-turned-actress by Jesse Lasky who, alerted to the girl's charms, signed her up for starlet training classes at Paramount's Astoria Studios in New York. Todd was a quick study and

Below: Cheerful comedienne Thelma Todd, 1932.

Above: A Los Angeles homicide captain examines the body of Thelma Todd.

Club. During the party, as she made her rounds, Todd ran into her ex-husband, Pat Di Cicco, and the two exchanged angry words. She also had a disconcerting discussion with theater owner Sid Grauman. Despite these flare-ups, guests said she left the party later in good spirits. Her chauffeur dropped her off out front of the café at about 4:00 A.M. on Sunday morning.

Sometime between that time Sunday morning and 10:00 A.M. Monday morning, Thelma Todd died. Her maid discovered her body, slumped over in the front seat of her car in the garage up the hill. The ignition was on, but the engine had stopped. There was blood spattered on the dead actress's face and coat. Several of her ribs were cracked. The coroner declared carbon monoxide poisoning as the cause of death.

The initial response by police and others was murder, as there was no note or motive for sui-cide. Others speculated that the death was an accident, that Todd had locked herself out of her apartment, had climbed the hill to sit in the car to keep warm, and that the fumes in the closed garage overcame her.

Speculation swirled through the film colony. It was well known that Todd had been con-cerned about gangsters and often told her chauffeur to drive faster to protect her from being kidnapped or killed by them. This was far from mere paranoia; evidence suggests that mob-ster Lucky Luciano wanted to establish a gambling room above the café but Todd had refused.

Adding another twist to the case were sev-eral "sightings" of Thelma Todd, all of which were at odds with the coroner's reported time of her death as 2:30 A.M. Sunday. Several prominent eyewitnesses testified to seeing her alive in her car with a handsome stranger Sunday morning at 10:00 A.M.; another witness said she received a phone call from Todd at 4:30 P.M. that same day, and a pharmacist swore he saw her make the call from his store!

Regardless of these apparent leads, before the week was out the murder theory had been rescinded by police and an "accidental" ruling was made (her ribs were supposed to have been

was one of the very few in the class to earn a Hollywood contract. She arrived in Hollywood and became almost an instant success, appearing opposite such comedy greats as the Marx Brothers and Laurel and Hardy.

By 1935 she was a star—bubbly, fresh, and fun-loving—but uncertain how long her star would shine (as were most stars of the day). Thinking of this, she invested in the half-owner-ship of a café on the Pacific Coast Highway with director Roland West. She and West (platonic friends) made their home above the cafe. West owned a home up the cliff behind the restaurant; Todd and West each parked their cars in the same garage.

Early in December 1935, comedian Stanley Lupino, father of actress Ida, threw a Saturday night party for Todd at the famous Trocadero

DEATH IN THE DESERT

In the summer of 1954, 220 Hollywood cast and crew members spent two months filming *The Conqueror* in the Utah desert near St. George. Of that number (as of 1981) ninety-one had contracted cancer and forty-six of those had died. The summer be-fore the film shoot, 137 miles (220 km) away at Yucca Flat, the government had con-ducted above-ground atomic testing. The lingering radia-tion had tragic effects on the film company, as well as the town of St. George.

Among the scores of people affected were Holly-wood legends Dick Powell, producer of the film (who died in 1963 of lymph cancer), star John Wayne

cracked when she fell against the steering wheel). It was widely speculated that evidence in the killing had been once again suppressed by the "powers-that-be" (the studios) in order to avoid scandal. There is plenty of evidence to support the claim; weeks after the death an anonymous telegram sent to the Los Angeles Police Department said that Thelma Todd's killer was holed up in a hotel room in Ogden, Utah. Los Angeles police never pursued the lead, claiming the case was closed.

Accident, suicide, or murder? Thanks to another deft and effective Hollywood cover-up, we'll never know the truth behind the death of actress Thelma Todd.

Perhaps no Hollywood mystery has aroused as much curiosity, speculation, sympathy, and scandal as Marilyn Monroe's death by apparent drug overdose.

The last few years of Monroe's life were filled with unhappiness. She had become a monster on the sets of her films; costar Tony Curtis remembered her for her "vicious arrogance" and "vindictive selfishness." She was unpleasant to everyone on the Fox lot from the lowliest grip to the highest production personnel.

By the time she began work on *Something's Got to Give*, the title had become prophetic. Monroe showed up on only a handful of shooting days, racking up astronomical cost overruns for the production. Fox canceled the picture and suspended her, sending the star into a brooding mood. She consulted her psychiatrist, Dr. Ralph Greenson, and constantly called her physician about a variety of disorders that were psychosomatic. She was afraid of absolutely everything in her life at the time: men, aging, her womanhood, the decline of her career, the insanity that ran in her family, and loneliness. A poem she wrote during this period was found in her papers after her death; it clearly spelled out her sense of helplessness:

Below: A hearse removes the body of Marilyn Monroe from her Brentwood bungalow, August 5, 1962.

(who died in 1979 after a long battle with lung, throat, and stomach cancer), and leading lady Susan Hayward (who died in 1975 after battling for years against skin, breast, and uterine cancers and brain tumors). Costar Agnes Moorehead made the connection between the fallout and the cancer cases before cancer killed her in 1974, saying, "Everybody in the picture has gotten cancer and died. I should never have taken that part." Executive producer Howard Hughes, who was on the set every day, may have become a famous recluse—never leaving his home, wearing white gloves—because of a serious bout with skin cancer, as opposed to the often cited, but highly improbable, "germ phobia."

True Grit

Help, help
Help, I feel life coming closer
When all I want is to die.

On August 4, 1962, Marilyn had dinner with her press agent, Pat Newcomb. During the meal, according to Eunice Murray, Monroe's live-in psychiatric nurse, she received a mysterious phone call which seemed to upset her. Newcomb left shortly afterward, and Monroe was said to have retired for the night.

Murray awoke in the night and was alarmed to find Monroe's light still on after midnight. She tried the door but it was locked; there was no response to her shouts. She called Greenson and together they broke a pane of glass in an outside French door and entered to find Monroe naked on the bed with the phone receiver clutched in her right hand. A bottle of strong barbiturates she had been prescribed that week was empty beside the bed. Marilyn Monroe was dead.

Immediately the scandal erupted, along with theories of conspiracy.

The primary focus was Monroe's connection to John and Robert Kennedy. Actor Peter Lawford, brother-in-law to the president, had introduced Monroe to John F. Kennedy and his brother Robert, the Attorney General of the United States. Rumors flew that Monroe had begun an affair with Jack Kennedy before he became president and that they had continued the affair while he was in the White House; others believed Bobby Kennedy was the one with whom Monroe had the affair; still others said she was the lover of both men. The "conspiracy theory" says that Monroe was "dangerous" to the political careers of the men and that they were somehow responsible for having her killed. Monroe had, in fact, kept a "little red diary," inside which she supposedly had written intimate details of the mob's plot to kill Fidel Castro and other "explosive" secrets. The "dangerous" diary disappeared from the actress's effects in the coroner's office.

Other theories hold that factions close to the Kennedys—such as the CIA, the FBI, or the mob—were behind her death, for various reasons. A variation on this conspiracy theory says that ene-

Opposite: Marilyn Monroe at home in Hollywood, 1952. Left: A friend of Marilyn and relative of the Kennedy family, actor Peter Lawford.

mies of the Kennedys ended Monroe's life "in such a way as to appear a suicide" over her affair with Jack Kennedy in order to exert right-wing pressure on the president.

It's hard to tell where reality ends and fantasy begins. Years after Monroe's death, her nurse Murray "confessed" that Bobby Kennedy had visited Monroe that fateful day and that the two had argued. Murray said that Monroe was tired of being "passed around like a piece of meat," and claimed that Monroe wanted to marry Bobby.

There was a two- to three-hour gap between the time Monroe's body was found and the arrival of the police. Peter Lawford reportedly went to the house on behalf of the Kennedys to locate and remove any evidence of their presence there. Again, this is secondhand knowledge, reported by Frank Otash, a private detective who says Lawford tried to hire him to do the job. The detective claims he refused and that Lawford decided to go through the house on his own.

Above: Natalie Wood.

Still, Hollywood continues to offer up mysteries, like the tragic and unexplained drowning of actress Natalie Wood in the waters off of Santa Catalina Island.

On a November day in 1981 Natalie Wood and her devoted husband Robert Wagner boarded their sixty-foot (18-m) yacht, *Splendour*, which was moored in a quiet cove off of the island. Natalie was looking forward to a weekend off from work on her latest feature film, *Brainstorm*, just three days from being completed on the East Coast. The couple was joined by Natalie's *Brainstorm* costar Christopher Walken.

The three actors and Dennis Davern, captain of the yacht, went ashore for dinner at an island restaurant. Customers at the restaurant noticed tensions were high between the three actors and sent over complimentary bottles of champagne to try and lighten their mood. Customers in the place overheard Wagner get upset about Wood's "flirting" with Walken.

Why would the happily married Wood flirt with Walken that weekend? Some theorized that Wood was upset over (untrue) rumors about Wagner having an affair with his *Hart to Hart* costar Stefanie Powers and hoped to get back at Wagner by inviting *her* costar along for the weekend and flirting with him. Later, when Wagner wanted to leave the restaurant, another argument ensued, for Wood wanted to stay and party. Eventually they came to an agreement and all left for the yacht together.

The tension between Wagner and his wife was still present when they arrived back at the yacht at about 10:30 P.M. Around midnight Wood left the main cabin for her stateroom. Walken retired to his stateroom as well. Wagner went to commiserate with Davern in his quarters.

At some point, Wood left her stateroom and went out on deck, dressed only in socks, a nightgown, and a down jacket. Despite her well-known fear of water, especially at night, she untied the rubber dinghy at the side of the yacht. No one knows what she was trying to do or what happened next, but somehow the forty-three-year-old actress slipped, jumped, or fell as she

Why did these people speak up so long after the event? Were they offering up legitimate pieces of the puzzle or were they simply looking for publicity? Was Marilyn Monroe's lonesome death the end result of a complex political conspiracy to hide the amorous adventures of America's top government officials, or was it simply the last act of a troubled and desperate woman who felt "life getting closer" when all she wanted was to die? Despite the mountain of books and articles written about Marilyn Monroe and her death that fateful night, the answers continue to elude us, the truth hidden in a whirl of conflicting statements and supposition.

Tragedy befell the four costars, the director, and the producer of the 1955 cult youth film.

James Dean, the troubled young star of the film, was the first to die, in an automobile accident on September 30, 1955. (See page 31.)

Sal Mineo, the handsome young costar, seemed to have a bright future ahead of him after garnering Academy Award nominations for *Rebel* and *Exodus*. But in the sixties and seventies his career all but stalled out; he was reduced to playing an ape in *Planet of the Apes*. On February 12, 1976, he was stabbed to death by a would-be robber outside his West Hollywood apartment.

Costar Nick Adams went on to star as Johnny Yuma in television's *The Rebel,* but he battled severe depression over marital difficulties with his troubled, neurotic wife. He committed suicide by ingesting paraldehyde—a tranquilizer prescribed for nervousness—and left no note.

Costar Natalie Wood drowned mysteriously off the coast of Santa Catalina Island in November 1981. (See page 154.)

Director Nicholas Ray died of lung cancer in 1979.

David Weisbard, who produced the film for Warner Brothers, died of a sudden "mysterious" illness at age forty-four.

handled the small boat, hitting her head and sliding beneath the water unconscious. She quickly drowned in the cold water.

Hours later, Wagner realized that Wood and the dinghy were gone. Thinking she had gone ashore in anger, he waited before alerting any authorities. Eventually a search began. Her body was found the next morning, floating just beneath the surface about a mile from the *Splendour.* The dinghy was just 200 yards (183 m) away. Her blood alcohol content was 0.14, well over the 0.10 mark of legal intoxication.

Immediately questions were raised. Why had a woman deathly afraid of water at night untied a dinghy and attempted to board it alone? If she was heading ashore to escape the tensions on board, why was she dressed the way she was? What really happened on board the *Splendour* that night between Walken, Wagner, and Wood?

Natalie Wood's death was pronounced an accidental drowning, but these questions continue even today to nag at friends and fans of Wood, a woman who seemed to have arrived at a happy plateau in life and yet who risked and lost it all off the coast of southern California for mysterious and still unknown reasons. Her story remains another baffling entry in the catalog of unsolved Hollywood mysteries.

Left: Robert Wagner's sixty-foot (18-m) yacht, Splendour, *near the sight of Natalie Wood's drowning.*

Bibliography

Adler, Bill. *Elizabeth Taylor: Triumphs and Tragedies.* New York: Ace Books, 1982.

Anger, Kenneth. *Hollywood Babylon.* San Francisco: Straight Arrow Books, 1975.

Arthur, Marx. *The Nine Lives of Mickey Rooney.* New York: Stein and Day, 1986.

Austin, John. *Hollywood's Unsolved Mysteries.* New York: Shapolsky Publishers, 1990.

Bainbridge, John. *Garbo.* Garden City, N.Y.: Doubleday and Co., 1955.

Barson, Michael S. *Judy, Liza, The Myth and the Madness.* Cresskill, N.J.: Sharon Publications, 1985.

Brown, Peter Harry. *Kim Novak: Reluctant Goddess.* New York: St. Martin's Press, 1986.

Brown, Peter H. *The Real Oscar: The Story Behind the Academy Awards.* Westport, Conn.: Arlington House Books, 1981.

_____ , and Jim Pinkston. *Oscar Dearest: Six Decades of Scandal, Politics, and Greed Behind Hollywood's Academy Awards, 1927–1986.* New York: Perennial Library, 1987.

Caine, Michael. *Michael Caine's Moving Picture Show.* New York: St. Martin's Press, 1988.

Carr, William H. A. *Hollywood Tragedy.* Greenwich, Conn.: Fawcett Publications, 1976.

Cini, Zelda, and Bob Crane. *Hollywood: Land and Legend.* Los Angeles: Rosebud Books, 1980.

Cohen, Daniel, and Susan Cohen. *Hollywood Hunks and Heroes.* New York: Simon & Schuster, 1985.

Consumer Guide, eds. *Movie Trivia Mania.* Skokie, Ill.: Publications International, Ltd., 1989.

Dalton, David. *James Dean, the Mutant King: A Biography.* San Francisco, Calif.: Straight Arrow Books, 1974.

David, Lester, and Jhan Robbins. *Richard and Elizabeth.* New York: Funk & Wagnalls, 1977.

Davidson, Bill. *Spencer Tracy, Tragic Idol.* New York: E. P. Dutton, 1987.

Davis, Daphne. *Stars!* New York: Stewart, Tabori & Chang, 1983.

Edwards, Anne. *Judy Garland.* New York: Simon & Schuster, 1975.

Edmonds, I.G. *Hollywood R.I.P.* Evanston, Ill.: Regency Books, 1963.

Eells, George. *Hedda and Louella.* New York: G. P. Putnam's Sons, 1972.

_____. *Robert Mitchum: A Biography.* New York: Franklin Watts, 1984.

_____ , and Stanley Musgrove. *Mae West: A Biography.* New York: William Morrow and Co., 1982.

Epstein, Edward Z., and Joe Morella. *Rita: The Life of Rita Hayworth.* New York: Delacorte Press, 1983.

Finch, Christopher, and Linda Rosenkrantz. *Gone Hollywood.* Garden City, N.Y.: Doubleday and Co., 1979.

Flynn, Errol. *My Wicked, Wicked Ways.* New York: G. P. Putnam's Sons, 1959.

Friedrich, Otto. *City of Nets: A Portrait of Hollywood in the 1940's.* New York: Harper & Row, 1986.

Gardner, Ava. *Ava, My Story.* New York: Bantam Books, 1990.

Graham, Sheilah. *The Garden of Allah.* New York: Crown Publishers, 1970.

Guiles, Fred Lawrence. *Legend: The Life and Death of Marilyn Monroe.* New York: Stein and Day, 1984.

Halliwell, Leslie. *The Filmgoer's Book of Quotes.* London: Hart-Davis, MacGibbon, 1973.

Hansen-Steiger, Sherry, and Brad Steiger. *Hollywood and the Supernatural.* New York: St. Martin's Press, 1990.

Harris, Warren G. *Gable and Lombard.* New York: Simon & Schuster, 1974.

_____ . *Natalie and R.J.: Hollywood's Star-Crossed Lovers.* New York: Doubleday, 1988.

Herndon, Venable. *James Dean: A Short Life.* Garden City, N.Y.: Doubleday and Co., 1974.

Higham, Charles. *Ava: A Life Story.* New York: Delacorte Press, 1974.

_____. *Bette: The Life of Bette Davis.* New York: Macmillan Publishing, 1981.

_____ , and Roy Moseley. *Cary Grant: The Lonely Heart.* New York: Harcourt Brace Jovanovich, Inc., 1989.

Kelley, Kitty. *His Way: The Unauthorized Biography of Frank Sinatra.* New York: Bantam Books, 1986.

Leff, Leonard J., and Jerold L. Simmons. *The Dame in the Kimono.* New York: Grove Weidenfeld, 1990.

Lewis, Jerry, with Herb Gluch. *Jerry Lewis, In Person.* New York: Atheneum, 1982.

McCann, Graham. *Marilyn Monroe.* New Brunswick, N.J.: Rutgers University Press, 1988.

McClelland, Doug. *Hollywood On Hollywood.* Winchester, Mass.: Faber and Faber, 1985.

Peary, Danny. *Close-ups.* New York: Workman Publishing, 1978.

Polanski, Roman. *Roman.* New York: William Morrow and Co., 1984.

Quirk, Lawrence J. *Fasten Your Seat Belts.* New York: William Morrow and Co., 1990.

Shulman, Irving. *Harlow: An Intimate Biography.* New York: Bernard Geis Associates, 1964.

Stallings, Penny, with Howard Mandelbaum. *Flesh and Fantasy.* New York: Harper and Row, 1978.

Starks, Michael. *Cocaine Fiends and Reefer Madness.* New York: Cornwall Books, 1982.

Stenn, David. *Clara Bow: Runnin' Wild.* Garden City, N.Y.: Doubleday and Co., 1988.

Street-Porter, Janet. *Scandal!* New York: Dell, 1983.

Tajiri, Vincent. *Valentino.* New York: Bantam Books, 1977.

Thomas, Bob. *Joan Crawford: A Biography.* New York: Simon & Schuster, 1978.

_____. *Marlon: Portrait of the Rebel as an Artist.* New York: Random House, 1973.

Torrence, Bruce T. *Hollywood: The First 100 Years.* Hollywood, Cal.: Hollywood Chamber of Commerce, 1979.

Turner, Lana. *Lana: The Lady, the Legend, the Truth.* New York: E. P. Dutton, 1982.

Wansell, Geoffrey. *Haunted Idol: The Story of the Real Cary Grant.* New York: William Morrow and Co., 1984.

Wayne, Jane Ellen. *Gable's Women.* New York: Prentice Hall, 1987.

Wilson, Colin, and Donald Seaman. *Scandal!* New York: Stein and Day, 1986.

Wolf, Marvin J., and Katharine Meder. *Fallen Angels: Chronicles of L.A. Crime and Mystery.* New York: Facts on File Publications, 1986.

Woodward, Bob. *Wired: The Short Life and Fast Times of John Belushi.* New York: Simon & Schuster, 1984.

Woodward, Ian. *Audrey Hepburn.* New York: St. Martin's Press, 1984.

Photo Credits

PRINCIPAL PHOTOGRAPHY BY:

© The Motion Picture & Television Photo Archive, pp. 8, 11, 12, 15-17, 19-21, 25-27, 30-48, 50, 54-55, 61, 63, 66, 67, 73, 79-82, 92, 93, 97-100, 102, 105, 106, 109, 111, 114, 116, 118, 119, 121, 125-130, 132, 133, 137, 138, 144, 154. Photos by George Hurrell, pp. 6, 56-57; photo by Ruth H. Louise, p. 22; photos by Laszlo Willinger, pp. 24, 142; photo by Scotty Welbourne, p. 29; photos by Paul Hesse, pp. 51, 120; photos by Richard Miller, pp. 52, 152; photo by Herb Ritts, p. 62; photos by Mac Julian, pp. 64, 107; photos by Sid Avery, pp. 83, 89, 124 bottom; photo by Gabi Rona, p. 101; photos by Clarence S. Bull, pp. 103, 122; photo by Ted Allan, p.124 top; photo by M. Marigold, p. 140.

ADDITIONAL PHOTOGRAPHY BY:

© Archive Photos, pp. 18, 77, 117, 131, 134, 136, 143 top & bottom.

© AP/Wide World Photos, pp. 60, 71, 76, 110, 112, 146, 147 top & bottom, 148, 150, 151, 155.

© FPG International, pp. 10, 13, 14, 23, 49, 53, 58, 68-70, 78, 85, 87, 88, 90-91, 123, 139, 149.

© Ron Galella Ltd.: photos by James Smeal, pp. 74, 75, 115, 145; Ron Galella, pp. 94, 153; Anthony Savignano, p. 96; Albert Ortega, p. 11.

Index